THE WELL
OF LIFE

GEORGES
CHEVROT

THE WELL
OF LIFE

Scepter

Contents

INTRODUCTION

The episode of the Samaritan woman in St. John's Gospel (Jn 4:1–42) is a passage that is most dear to those familiar with the Gospel. In a wonderful short sketch, St. John lays before our eyes the whole personality of our Lord Jesus Christ, the Man so far above us, and the God so close to us.

All the tenderness in the heart of Jesus is revealed in the unforgettable appeal by which he shows us the need that he feels to give himself to us. And how can we resist his advances, when we see how they transform the heart of man?

Here we see the immediate and unexpected conversion of a woman who gives up indifference and sin in order to become the Savior's apostle. Here we see a crowd of her compatriots who, in the space of a few hours, passes through all the stages of life. Here, in the background, are the Lord's first disciples who are preparing for the time when the gospel must be sown.

No one will ever exhaust all the riches of this episode in the life of Jesus. We, no more than anyone else, can claim to have done so. In these pages you will thus find neither an academic commentary on the thought of the sacred writer nor any strict sequence among the subjects. I have simply followed St. John's text, verse by verse, trying to extract from it some useful thoughts and images.

Monsignor Georges Chevrot,
Paris, France

1

TIRED

> Jacob's well was there, and so Jesus, wearied as he was with his journey, sat down beside the well. It was about the sixth hour. (John 4:6)

Jesus and his disciples had been more or less compelled to leave Judea, and were returning to Galilee by the quickest, but most difficult, route which crossed the mountains of Samaria. It was about midday, time to halt.

The little group stopped near the town of Sichar, near a memorable well that had been there since Jacob's time.

Jesus and his disciples had been walking since morning. The Lord let his disciples go to the town for provisions.

We should thank the Evangelist for showing us the Savior so tired. His weariness should help us to bear our own. One of the invocations in the Litany of the Holy Name of Jesus asks for deliverance through the Savior's weariness: *Per labores tuos, libera nos, Domine.*

In this wearied Savior, tired humanity can see itself. Leaning against the well, Jesus had just stretched himself out as he did during his hour of rest when he was a young working man in Nazareth, just like any young worker at any period in any country who sits down on the ground for a few minutes before going back to the job.

Without a doubt, work is the crown on our brow: it is the joy of producing, of creating. Whether we have a pen or a tool in our hand, it is always our spirit which is in command, and by our work, we come closer to the spirit of God. But work is also the sweat on our brow, the tension of our brain, the strain on our back. It is the first insufficient attempt that has to be done over again and corrected, the sadness of not being able to achieve what the mind has conceived, the arms that fall down exhausted. Like us, the Son of God felt this bitter moment when the body escapes from the mastery of the will.

Nor, because of its rarity, is this an exceptional episode which the Evangelist notes. Jesus fell asleep in the boat that was tossed and shaken by the sudden storm on the Sea of Galilee. Like us, Jesus was often worn out at the end of tiresome days. Like his, our tiredness has something divine in it, provided it is not the exhaustion of a dissipated life, but the price of a life spent in the service of others and in the performance of duty.

Christians, let us think of our tired Savior when our job forces us to sit up late after a day of over-work. Christian women, wives, mothers, housekeepers, whose work never finishes, when you get up in the morning more tired than when you were going to bed, think of your tired Christ.

But even more to be pitied are those without work. Did not Jesus suffer, at Sichar, that vain despairing tiredness of the unemployed? Rejected by orthodox Judea, he was walking uselessly through heretical Samaria, not a soul to convert. Worn out, he sat down at the side of the well.

Let us also, you and I, lay down by the side of Jacob's well all the weariness in our soul. But first and foremost, let us lay down our soul itself, which is so often a burden to us. Oscillating without rest between great heights and abysmal depths, we are never the same person from one hour to the next; and how exhausting that is!

Next comes our will, which is so easily weakened in the struggle against our faults, as well as in our efforts to practice virtue. The results are always so far behind our desires! We are truly itinerants, working and looking for work along an endless road, in the dust and under the sun. *Hora erat quasi sexta* (It was about noon). It is only noon! We will still have to trudge on until evening, *fatigatus ex itinere* (wearied as he was with his journey).

Let us be reassured. When it comes to our moral weariness, the Lord does not look on these things in the same way as we do; he sees in them so many victories. Let us not overrate ourselves and ignore our weakness in order to play the hero. We shall resemble the Son of Man when we content ourselves with being his creatures, capable only of limited, interrupted, and intermittent efforts.

Let us not fool ourselves any longer by imagining that the piety that God asks of us requires intelligence that is always keen, feelings that are always on the alert, and a heart that is ever enthusiastic. It is quite normal that our piety should sometimes become monotonous and not very attractive. That is hard on us, certainly, but God is not in the least offended. He accepts our prayers even when we are very sleepy; he accepts our worship even when we are distracted; he even accepts also the sorrow we feel at not knowing how to speak to him as we would like.

Does a remedy exist, if not for all our tiredness, at least for our spiritual weariness? There can be none other than that which Jesus proposed by his example. Like him, let us learn to live with our tiredness.

Certainly, tiredness is a fetter on our activity; above all, it is detrimental to the quality of our actions. When we are tired, we do less, and what we do is done less well.

Can you avoid tiredness? Do everything possible, at least, to lessen it. Make a judicious choice among the tasks that occupy you. Distinguish between what is essential and what is only accessory, eliminate everything in your life which is only a concession to your own caprice, to vanity, to fashion.

But I know that after this elimination, which will give you a little extra time, you will still not reap the benefit of it. You will only devote yourself still more to your professional, family and social duties. Your time will be taken up by more serious tasks, but you will still be completely busy. And then, it is not for you, but for another Master, to decide the questions of your health, the illness of those whom you love, events which will impose new duties on you. True Christians will always tire themselves out.

But, you will object, this lessens your value, your power to produce, your apostolic possibilities, even your interior life. Not at all. It is, on the contrary, because you produce more that you are more tired. And your tiredness is an inexhaustible source of sanctification. Understand that here I speak only of tiredness that resembles Christ's tiredness and which we can offer to him. Such tiredness brings us to the very heart of religion.

What truer testimony of our love can we give to God than to use our strength to the limit in the fulfillment of our duty? What more complete, and at the same time more humble, gift can we make than to offer him in the morning all the toils and weariness that we shall feel during the day?

Does your tiredness prevent you from devoting yourself fully to your children's needs or from giving yourself to apostolic works? Rest assured that God will make it his business to see to the matters that you cannot look after. The least attended of your children will develop their initiative and personal efforts first and most strongly. If you yourself cannot come to the help of an invalid or a poor person, God will send someone who will do it better than you.

A SCHOOL OF HUMILITY

It is a blessed tiredness that teaches us not to want to do everything by ourselves, to rely primarily on God, and to make up for our inabilities by fervent prayer.

Tiredness is a school of humility which strengthens the bonds of fraternity among men. If we are all more or less tired, is it not, as St. Paul advises, in order that we may bear one another's burdens? Today we console our neighbor; tomorrow we shall ask for his help. And, because of this, we shall love each other more. Have you noticed that indefatigable people do not always know how to sympathize with the troubles of others?

Tiredness also entices us to detachment by preventing us from accomplishing what we would have liked to do. This multiplies our opportunities for hidden penances by which we can make reparation for all the guilt or insufficiency in our past actions.

To live with one's tiredness is to accept it, but also to make allowances for it. Let us imitate the divine Son of Man. He was tired, so he sat down. Let us moderate our activity so as to divide it properly among all those obligations which God assigns to us, so as not—for want of moderation—to fall into a paralyzing state of physical exhaustion or nervous prostration. Or even into a state of irritation or bad humor which lessens the value of our actions and makes us unbearable to others.

To live with one's tiredness means to accept bravely the life that God grants us, including the duties with which he fills it and the weaknesses to which he condemns us. It means that we never complain of our inabilities. We tire ourselves by living, without ever growing tired of life. Besides, the tiredness that God allows is never useless.

So let us go back to the well. Jesus is exhausted from so much walking without being able to do any work. And as he sits there, his heavy eyelids closed, a woman approaches across the fields on her way to get some water. Jesus opens his eyes again; he reads the soul of this sinner. His Father has thus blessed his tiredness. He sends him work, a creature to raise up again, a soul to save.

It is only on the other side of the grave that we shall know for how many sinners our tiredness, when offered to God, has meant salvation. Only then shall we see that our forced inactivity, like all our sufferings, may have been more fruitful for others than our actual services.

It was not only by the tortures of his Passion that he redeemed us. His work of redemption began at the very moment of his Incarnation. It was accomplished through the crying of the little Infant in the stable at Bethlehem, and it continued in the workshop at Nazareth. Jesus worked, preached, tired himself for our sake, before dying for us. He redeemed us by accepting, as we must, the daily miseries of our life.

Quaerens me sedisti lassus. (You were searching for me.) In order to seek me, Lord, you tired yourself so much that you could no longer stand up. I have tired you by these promises of mine which I forget so quickly, by my repeated faults after your loving forgiveness, by my neglects without number, by my unwillingness to follow you, by my excess of self-love.

And still you offer me all your help: your indulgences, your light, your grace, your rewards, your punishments. And you never grow weary of calling me, waiting for me, loving me! *Tantus labor non sit cassus!* (May your toil not be in vain!) Lord, may it not be that in seeking me you should tire yourself in vain.

2

PROVIDENTIAL MEETINGS

There came a woman of Samaria to draw water.
(John 4:7)

"Once one has met Jesus Christ," wrote J. B. Henri Lacordaire, "it is an intoxication which never ends."

Do you remember the day you met him for the first time? But that is a bad way of putting it, for every time we really meet him, it seems as if it were for the first time. One day it is his light which dazzles us; then it is his purity which seduces us. Then his generous forgiveness overwhelms us. And what can one say of those meetings at the Eucharistic banquet, where he gives himself to us completely and we try to give ourselves to him with equal generosity? And the meetings on our paths of sorrow, when he puts his cross on our shoulders and says to us: Redeem your brothers.

In order not to meet him, one would have to avoid him deliberately, for he declared: "I am with you always, to the close of the age" (Mt 28:20).

In this meeting that took place at Jacob's well, many a converted sinner will be deeply moved to find his own story. And are we not all "poor sinners" and always being converted and reconverted?

The teaching that the Lord offers us in this episode goes beyond those actual moments in which Jesus finds a way into our heart in order to move us to repentance. He is revealing to us something of those mysterious *meetings of grace*, in which we are object and instrument.

A Samaritan woman came. While Jesus is resting, the Samaritan woman comes toward the spring with an easy gait, her dress gathered into a linen waistband. She carries a jar on her shoulder, and her bracelets and necklaces jangle as she moves. A perfume of cinnamon and cassia surrounds her, and her eyes, shaded with kohl, meet the gaze of the stranger sitting near the well.

The moment he saw her in the distance, the Lord penetrated the depths of her conscience. Shortly afterwards, when the disciples return from Sichar, the Evangelist shows them to us quite dumbfounded to catch the Lord in conversation with this woman. Her appearance tells one immediately what she is, a sinner.

She came to draw water. How often before has she made this journey, just one of her daily occupations! What is she thinking? She's probably thinking about the unimportant work of her household. Does she show any curiosity upon seeing the stranger whom she is approaching? In any case, she is thinking about anything except what is in store for her.

Whose, then, is the invisible hand which regulates our comings and goings? Why do we leave our house at such an hour rather than at another? And why, when we go out, do we turn to the right rather than to the left? A delay of a quarter of an hour, and fortune passes us by. An unforeseeable incident is the beginning of a lasting friendship. In one minute, we avoid an accident, and in another, we fall. Every life contains many meetings that are decisive, for good or evil.

Is there someone who, at a given moment, causes those events which up-end life?

For the Christian, there is no question of chance in it. The uncertain outcomes between humans and the events they face cannot be excluded from God's providence. Yet, another difficulty arises. If the Father in heaven willed that the Samaritan woman should at that time and date meet the Savior who was to enlighten her spirit and liberate her flesh, could that same divine Father also bear responsibility for the times that this woman committed her misdeeds?

FREEING OURSELVES FROM EVIL

Let us believe rather in the Old Testament imagery, in which knowledge of Good and Evil hang on branches of the same tree. We cannot have one without the other. The same fact can be the occasion of good or of evil. On the same night, on the same street across the Tiber, two men pass: a young Roman is caught in the trap which is laid for him, while Ignatius of Loyola decides to open a homeless shelter. The same circumstance reveals the sinner and the saint. God wants our life to be a voluntary progress, a free ascent toward what is good. But we can only arrive at good by freeing ourselves from evil.

Let us have confidence, then, in God who guides us in our uncertainties. If some meeting has been unfortunate, we should not bewail it more than our own weakness or imprudence. That sinner who led us astray, did he not come our way so that we might help *him* to leave his sinful ways? And in the evening, when we are going over the events of the day, do we remember the day's good encounters and thank God?

If we are alert, not a day will pass in which we shall not meet sanctity in one form or another.

There came a woman of Samaria to draw water. Undoubtedly this woman has not the slightest notion of being converted. The cautious discussion in which she engages with Jesus at first bears no resemblance to a confession.

But what do we really know about it? Can one know what goes on in another's mind, however settled they may appear in life?

It would show little knowledge of human nature to presume that a sinner who one believes to be hardened does not suffer because of his or her state. In the intervals between his relapses is he not sometimes seized by disgust? Has he not tried, if not to raise himself up again, at least to take himself out of his habitual misery? Has no hand taken hold of his to help him?

And why should we accuse of pride the man who says, "I do not see God"? He says he does not believe, but is he still quite sure of his disbelief? Perhaps he is still searching, but in the wrong direction; he has not yet found the path which leads to light, therefore he continues to deny the light. But the pain of one who is seeking the truth, like the sorrow of one who sighs after virtue, is itself a prayer which is heard by God and to which, one unexpected day, he will give a victorious answer.

That is why the conversation with the Samaritan woman should not surprise us. Some people are scandalized on the pretext that it shows salvation under too easy a light. We cannot know what struggles may take place in the hearts of those who externally are separated from God. What we do know for certain is that any appeal, however weak, however hesitant, is always heard by God.

He hears it, and he reveals himself. How right it is to entrust blindly to him the salvation of sinners and unbelievers.

It is infinitely preferable to pray with confidence over a long period for the person about whom we are worried. And suddenly, under the influence of grace, the person surrenders. He simply recognizes his Savior and kneels before him.

Our daily life puts us in the way of many meetings, the majority of which are completely unforeseen. Do we prepare for the unexpected? We should never be caught off guard by it. Nor should we let any of the opportunities that it offers us escape.

The unforeseen meeting may perhaps be some danger waiting for us. Will we say the right thing or will we say something imprudent? Will our reflexes save us or will they enslave us? Jesus, foreseeing all the perils that lie in wait for us, advises us to combine the wisdom of the serpent with the simplicity of the dove. We should always have our hand held out ready to give, but should also have our eye open for any snares that may suddenly appear in our path.

But with those people whom Providence leaves in contact with us for a longer time, let us not miss the chance of spiritual exchanges. In these meetings, we gather something of the richness of their ideals, their observations, and their experiences. For our part, let us open up our own treasures to them.

After all, Jesus, worn out as he was, had every right to get some rest. If he had been silent in the Samaritan woman's presence, we would have known nothing about it, although his grace could easily have caught up with her later.

In the preceding chapter of his Gospel, St. John reports the conversation that the Lord had with the timid Nicodemus: this man had taken up his whole night. The Samaritan woman is now going to rob him of his much-needed afternoon rest. But is not consoling a soul that is in doubt and reconciling a sinner with God the best way to rest?

Let us imitate Jesus and allow no meeting to be without profit for those who approach us. We always have something to give: a little joy and a lot of hope, a little truth and a lot of humility, a little courage and plenty of patience. As Christians, we always have Christ to give.

doing her work by herself. There would be nothing left for us but to go and sit down a little farther off.

Jesus was much more tactful than that. You may say that it would have been shocking to see the Lord fussing about this creature, taking her vessel from her hands. Not, however, that Jesus would have seen anything humiliating in this attitude. He humiliated himself much more when he wanted to wash his apostles' feet. Jesus knew what the woman's reaction would be, and that an imprudent advance would have ruined his plan.

So, instead of giving his help, he asks a favor: *Give me a drink.* These were the divine tactics. Could she refuse a little water to a traveler parched by the midday sun? The "adversary" who asks for a favor disarms himself; at least, he obliges himself to the other, he gives the other an advantage over him.

Let us get to the bottom of the Master's intentions. Instead of saying to this woman, who believes that she is despised: "Woman, let us put an end to these traditional quarrels; I only wish you well," he gives her the chance to show him some kindness.

"I am not on speaking terms with so and so," one often hears, "it is better that way." No, it is not better, for silence petrifies and consolidates the misunderstanding. If one gives the cement time to set, it will be very difficult to break it. It is better to speak. But there is a way of doing it: Jesus' way is a good one. Explanations can come later. The conversation with the Samaritan woman must first begin. The gap must be bridged, the broken thread must be knotted again, and in order to do so, one must talk of everything but the subject of the disagreement.

Did the divine traveler consider his incalculable dignity, his infinite sanctity? Who was this woman beside him? It was he, nevertheless, who was the first to speak, and he obliged himself to her. When it is a question of wiping out a hatred or bringing about a reconciliation, he who makes the advances, far from being lowered, is the one who is truly great.

Jesus does not recognize enemies; but he does recognize sin. On the eve of the great drama, he cannot bear the horror of it; and the garden of Gethsemane witnesses the disgust and the suffering that the wickedness of sinners inflicts on him. But he suffers for us much more than for himself. Because sin is our greatest misfortune, his mercy urges him to save the sinner. Here again, it is necessary that the sinner should not refuse him entry to her heart. How is one to introduce truth into a conscience that the habit of evil has darkened? Can one speak of God to someone who lives outside his laws?

Perhaps this was the case with the woman of Sichar. Jesus wants her to repent, without speaking to her yet about her faults; he wants her to turn to God without pronouncing yet the name of him whom she has offended. That is why he says to her: *Give me a drink.*

PENETRATING SOULS

He has her perform an act of charity. If only she is compassionate, this tiny act of pity will bring her close to God. In the depths of this miserable soul, under all the instincts for which she is perhaps not entirely responsible, there is still some human feeling. It is this feeling that Jesus arouses.

The Savior's reasoning is never wrong. He would have gained nothing by rebuking her for her long misconduct. But he is going to win her over by reminding her that, after all, she has a good heart. Even if she has done a lot of bad things, she is still capable of doing a little good.

Let us learn from Jesus that most difficult art of penetrating into souls that seem to be hermetically sealed against divine grace. To try to force an entry would be to risk seeing it close up for ever. Sometimes this can happen to the conscience of someone we love, of a person we respect. But to whom can we not say like the Savior, *Give me a drink*? In order to prepare or to hasten a soul's return to God, let us get him to perform many acts of charity. In this way, we put him on the path of truth where, of course, good books or persuasive apologists will solve some of his intellectual doubts.

Now, to the extent that we do good, we quash our selfishness, which is the most persistent obstacle between God and us. Anyone who is charitable toward everybody is already living partially as a Christian. He cannot fail to admire and love Jesus, the model of all charity. Love of the poor is a step towards Eucharistic communion. Whoever fulfills the great dogma of human brotherhood is not far from adoring his heavenly Father.

But why limit this experience to a few? We who wish to preserve our faith at any price should not let our enthusiasm abate. We want to grow in union with God. Frédéric Ozanam, the founder of the Society of St. Vincent de Paul, sought to prove the vitality of Catholicism so that the exercise of charity would protect the faith of young Catholic students from an anti-Catholic public opinion.

The way that leads all unfailingly to God is the way of charity. It is the material gift which detaches us from ourselves, the forbearance which earns us the divine forgiveness for our own sins, the goodness, patience, and generosity which make us breathe in an atmosphere of God, in which we very soon meet him face-to-face.

Behind that stranger or friend who asks us for a drink, let us, humble Samaritans, not fail to see him who knocks on the door of our hearts only to pour into them the living water of eternal life.

4

PREJUDICE

The Samaritan woman said to him, "How is it that you, a Jew, ask a drink of me, a woman of Samaria?" For Jews have no dealings with Samaritans. (John 4:9)

The thirsty traveler has asked for a little cold water. The woman's instinctive reaction would be either to offer him her pitcher immediately or else to turn her back on him completely. Good village woman that she is, she neither refuses nor consents. She must satisfy her curiosity by making this foreigner speak, satisfying her self-esteem by making him see that, after all, one sometimes does have need of these cursed Samaritans. "For Jews have no dealings with Samaritans." *Non coutuntur.* Literally, no dealings, the final word in collective antipathies, one which eliminates the need for any further explanation.

Why do the two peoples hate each other? The Assyrians conquered Samaria seven centuries earlier and repopulated it with their immigrants. These pagan colonists adopted the religion and customs of the Hebrew

natives. But, on their return from Babylon, the true
Israelites had refused to recognize God's people in this
mixed population. Under the blow of this insult, the
Samaritans retorted by erecting a temple on Mount Gerizim to rival the one in Jerusalem.

Notice the phrase: *Non coutuntur Judaei cum Samarita-
nis.* (Jews have no dealings with Samaritans.) The woman
is convinced that the fault is with the others. Could she
think otherwise? She never considered whether her people had provoked their anger. It is the Jews who do not
want to have relations with *them*. Both sides are convinced
of the other's evil dispositions. In fact, the hatred that the
Jews feel for the Samaritans is extremely keen and bitter.

Centuries later, we cannot appreciate Jesus's audacity
when he tells the parable of the good Samaritan. Notice
that when he asked the scribe, "Which of these three, in
thy opinion, was neighbor to him that fell among the rob-
bers?" the scribe was slow to admit the truth: "He that
showed mercy to him." On no account would he have
soiled his lips with the word "Samaritan." Not even their
name is spoken.

The Samaritan woman is quite convinced that this
Jewish traveler is deviating from the contemptuous pride
of his compatriots only because he is tortured by thirst.
She cannot know that the whole purpose of Jesus' coming is precisely to break down the barriers behind which
human beings sincerely hate one another.

But how is it that even after the Savior's message, as
before, men continue to establish themselves in adverse
groups, to mistrust one another and to attribute the worst

motives to each other? So people widen the barriers that separate them from their fellow humans and erect obstacles that do not allow them to unite again. Why? *Non coutuntur.* If they do not speak to each other, they will never understand one another.

Isolated behind their barriers as they are, will people finally hear Jesus' appeal to this foreign woman? If we were only spectators, we could decide simply that fratricidal hatred will disappear only when mankind does. But can we forget that our Lord entrusted us with the task of spreading charity all over the world?

Each of us can make a breach in the wall which hides us from our fellow humans. Instead of adding a stone to these new towers of Babel, we can take one away every day if, in all circumstances, we are animated by the spirit of Jesus Christ.

Let us learn from the lesson of history. The nineteenth century erected a thick wall between the world of capital and that of labor, making enemies of two forces which need one another. On one side, suspicion; on the other, envy: on both sides, mutual lack of understanding.

Let us never avoid the society of those of our brothers who see the interests of our country under a different light from us. Let us begin by taking stock of what unites us instead of squabbling over what divides us. The grounds for agreement are so much vaster than those for disagreement. As regards a Catholic who is not entirely in agreement with us on human problems, let us perform this elementary act of charity of regarding him neither as weak-minded nor as a traitor.

Let us do more. Let us peaceably discuss with him the question that separates us. Let us try to understand his views honestly. If he also makes a corresponding effort, we shall be brought a little closer. And even if we each keep our original conviction, at least we shall have learned to respect one another, and shall bring to the defense of our ideas, perhaps more light, and certainly the persuasive strength of greater charity.

5

THE GIFT OF GOD

> Jesus answered her, "If you knew the gift of God, and who it is that is saying to you, 'Give me a drink,' you would have asked him, and he would have given you living water." (John 4:10)

J esus does not let himself be upset by the woman's discourteous reply. She has replied, and that is something. But he takes good care not to fall into the trap which she is laying for him: discussing the mutual grievances of their two nations. Since she seems curious to know why he did not hesitate to ask a favor of her, Jesus is going to excite her curiosity further. Does she know who it is who has asked her for a drink and that he, moreover, can give her living water?

If you knew the gift of God! Jesus says much with few words: The water that I am asking of you is itself a gift from God to humanity. You come here to fill your pitcher several times a day, and it seems quite natural to you to find the precious water without which you could not live. Have you ever reflected that it is God who makes

26

it run for you underneath the earth, sheltered from the burning sun?

Jesus knows how to talk to men and women. He seeks them out in their daily occupations, he takes advantage of their most insignificant thoughts to raise their spirit suddenly toward eternal realities. He finds the right moment to slip into the conversation, very quietly, very gently, the sentence that puts us in God's presence.

You know very well that the water I am asking you to share with me is yours, true enough, but it belongs first to God. You must know, woman of Samaria, that *God is he who gives,* who gives us everything, who is always giving! If you knew how he gives, with what generosity, without calculation, without taking his gift back, without your deserving it! He gives you water, wheat, the vine, the wool of the sheep, yes—but much more than that, for man does not live on bread alone. If only you knew all that he can give! If only you knew that *God gives himself* and to what extent he gives himself, for he who is asking you for a drink is, in a unique way, the gift of God.

This is "the gift of God," this is his reply to humanity which is always stretching out its hands at the edge of the impassable abyss. God shows himself at last. *Et homo factus est* (And became man).

Reflect on this. God has revealed himself through man, through the mechanism of a human life. A marvel, but one above all which disconcerts our *heart.* Can we understand that God loves us to the point of coming to live among us? *Si scires donum Dei!* (If only you knew the gift of God.) In Jesus, God and man meet.

Before the Passion, one of his apostles pronounced the eternal prayer of all religious souls: "Lord, show us the Father." Jesus answers him: "Have I been with you so long, and yet you do not know me, Philip? He who has seen me has seen the Father." (Jn 14:8–9).

Philip's question is easily understood. He would have liked to see the "God of the philosophers and scholars," God the creator and ruler of the worlds, God who would enlighten us on all the secrets of nature. Jesus has revealed God to us, not less immense, but less aloof from us, God the author, animator, and end of our life, God as man here below can understand him. He has revealed everything that man needs to know about God.

In Jesus, we have seen the sanctity, the justice, the goodness of God. It is easy from now on to love God, to speak to him, to understand him, for Jesus—our interpreter—can be the object of our affections. It is he who prays for us and who brings us the Father's answer.

In Jesus, all contradictions are reconciled. He brings into harmony the justice and mercy of God, his sanctity and love. For the same God who cannot stand the offense of sin is now the Man of Sorrows who expiates all men's faults.

We contemplate God on the Cross, in the very act of taking away our sins, defeated, exhausted like us by suffering, conquered by death. But the defeat is only apparent and temporary. Jesus rises and takes us with him into his glory, for he is "the Resurrection and the Life" (Jn 11:25).

Do we understand now the gift of God? When God gives, he gives infinitely, without limit. He never takes back what he gives. In Jesus, divinity is unity with humanity *forever*: "God became man," says St. Augustine, "so that man might become God" (Serm. 128). His Father is our Father. Having received Jesus we have been made sons of God (Jn 1:12). We are not his children in name only, we are, in fact (1 Jn 3:1).

When Jesus leaves our earth, he gives us the peace which preserves his life in us. He fills our hearts with his spirit. And he himself, now invisible once more, is with us all days even to the end of the world (Mt 28:20).

He alone satisfies the desires and complaints of his believers. In his presence, our reason is no longer aggressive, it ceases to demand proofs from the divinity, for our pride disappears before the Son of God who—with the exception of sin—has shared our suffering. We unburden our sins and rise again, sure of divine forgiveness.

In his presence, our conscience is purified and our will is strengthened. In his presence, we take courage again, knowing that our life has an aim, that our earth is moving toward heaven, that united with the Son of God, we too, like him, shall leave the world and go to the Father. (Jn 16:28).

Si scires. We know this, but not well enough to live it. What happiness, what hope, what strength we should draw from our faith every day! Truly, in giving us Jesus, God gave us everything!

6

WHO IT IS

If you knew the gift of God and who it is that is saying to you, "Give me a drink," you would have asked him, and he would have given you living water. (John 4:10)

J esus is the revelation of God. The name *Emmanuel* by which Isaiah heralded him is explained in St. Matthew's text: *quod est interpretatum: Nobiscum Deus,* literally, "Which means: God with us!"

With us, with mankind. Not for the vain purpose of affirming his existence did he take our nature, but to put himself within our reach. We are out of our depth once we try to grasp God in his infinite being. Therefore, he came down to our level so as to communicate to us, bestowing not a complete knowledge of himself, but a human knowledge, incomplete, yet in conformity with the truth. Through Jesus, we know what God is for us, what he intends for us, what he expects of us.

If we understood this gift of God properly, and that Jesus is calling us to share in the divine life, our demand

would coincide with his own. We would beg him to
us to live as children of God.

In Jesus Christ, the two natures form a single person
in such a unity that the solder which joins them cannot
be seen. Jesus is fully God and also fully man. He teaches
us both the human knowledge of God, and the divine
knowledge of man, in showing man as God conceives
him and wishes him to be. Christ is our brother without
sin, you will object. Yes, without sin, because it is not
essential to sin in order to be a man.

Jesus is the pledge and object of our eternity, the price
of our redemption, and our spiritual food, but he is also
our everyday companion. As he is the revelation of God,
he is also the revelation of man. As man, he can reveal
to us what we are, not because he was a good and just
man whom the admiration of his fellows later defined,
but because he is God made man.

Among all the titles by which we know him, Jesus
obviously preferred "Son of Man"; in fact, he himself is
the only one to use that title. Neither the multitude nor
the disciples ever call him by it. He liked to call himself
the Son of Man, and in him we have indeed the most
noble human model that could exist.

How consoling it is to consider our humanity
through him! Certainly, since Jesus' time, and more and
more according as the gospel has spread, the number of
individuals who are a credit to the race has increased,
and it would be impossible to count all those humble
people whose virtue places them above the average. May
our holy model be blessed for showing them the way!

But for all our fellow creatures in whom we find cause for praise, how many disgust us with our nature, which in them displays so much animality, savagery, and hideousness! Are they responsible for their malice? We are sometimes seized with anger at the extremes of nastiness of which people show themselves capable. Should they then be regarded as senseless brutes? This would mean to despair of the intelligence and the future of our race.

As for ourselves, who like to be classed among the not-so-bad, are we not discouraged at the weaknesses of our character? Let us not give up hope. Man in himself is not as wicked or as mediocre as all that. The true man, the real man, is Jesus, and the more we try to resemble him, the more we are truly men, beings possessed of integrity, courage, and goodness.

Let us look at the Son of Man: his perfection will make us more indulgent toward those who fall, and more patient with ourselves. We are not only the sons of Adam and Cain, we are also the brothers of Christ, who has regenerated our race and made it healthy again. We have in us, not merely the seeds of all sorts of sins, but also greatness, the will to do good, because, as St. Paul says, Christ is being formed in us (Gal 4:19). Grace is fashioning our soul "to the measure of the stature of the fullness of Christ" (Eph 4:13).

Just as Jesus shows us God, so he also shows us man—what he is, what he ought to be, and what he can be.

"If he boasts, I humble him; if he humbles himself, I exalt him and contradict him forever, until he understands that he is an incomprehensible monster." For these harsh words, let us forgive the severe genius of philosopher Blaise Pascal, who is speaking here only of man without God. But the gospel has definitely thrown light on the mystery of man.

What is man? We cannot learn the answer from the long history of idolatrous humanity, which shows the same picture in every age: the strong oppressing the weak, reducing them to serfdom, with only death re-establishing equality between those who enjoyed life and those who suffered through it.

Nor are philosophies any more instructive. Some exalt man's pride, others invite him to seek wisdom in contemplation or rest in oblivion. Some proclaim his basic good, others regard him as the slave of his passions.

But what is man? Angel or beast? The faithful of the Old Testament were better informed, for they knew that man was slime of the earth and, at the same time, the breath of God. But Jesus has defined our exact status for us, and we can no longer be in any doubt as to what man is and how great is his dignity.

He has the dignity of a son, conceived by the love of his Father in heaven who is always attentive to his needs; exiled, but traveling toward his Father's house; a son who must obey his Father, but toward whom the Father is also bound; a son, therefore an heir (Gal 4:7), who will be the owner of all that the Father possesses. And the Father is already watching for the return of his lost son, ready to put on his finger the ring of nobility. He says to his faithful child, "All that is mine is yours" (Lk 15:31).

From now on, he is going "to make his abode with the son who loves him and keeps his word" (Jn 14:23).

Although none of the duties of which Jesus has given us an example is theoretically impossible to us, in practice, many cannot fulfill them all or cannot fulfill them always. The conscience says, "You ought," but the will replies, "I cannot," and afterwards, when the fault has been committed, the reason says, "I should have."

THE DUTY OF THE NORMAL MAN

For this sad fact of experience, some people say that there are only two possible explanations: that our nature keeps us in a state of revolt or it keeps us in a condition of impotence. In either case, we would have to conclude that Jesus and we do not belong to the same race. But the Son of Man, as we know him, does not allow us to accept this conclusion.

Because Jesus could carry out every duty, we cannot exclude him from humanity. On the contrary, it is by seeing all the good that he accomplished that we know what should be the duty of the normal man. Since Jesus lived among us, he revealed to us all the good of which man is capable. He knows the perfection toward which he is obliged to tend. Since Jesus' time, we can no longer give way to the evil inclinations of our nature without being conscious that we are sinning, or falling below our true nature. Since Jesus showed how a man can live, we will have no peace unless we reproduce the type of humanity that he has shown us.

But now it remains to give some acc
ficulties we must surmount in order t
which otherwise prevent us from imita
only two explanations, revolt or powerlessn
imputable to our nature? On this point, the Son of Man
consoles and encourages us. Neither our revolts, he shows
us, nor our weaknesses, are part of our true nature.

If human nature were powerless to fulfill its duty,
we would be the victims of some evil determinism. We
would no longer be sons, but galley slaves doomed to
lifelong punishment.

On the other hand, if our nature itself made us rebels,
we would always be guilty. It is not true that we are only
criminals, for we are also capable of loving God and desir-
ing what is good. What kind of father would have children
whose only resemblance to him was so radically different
that it condemned them to being disowned? In that case,
we would not be guilty at all, for we were given our nature.

KNOWING OUR TRUE SELVES

In bemoaning our nature, we follow the wrong path.
We misconceive the spirit with which our Father ani-
mates us, his children. Jesus taught us to know our better self which is our true self. He makes us take notice
of everything that is good in us. The example of his
all-holy person illumines our soul, which we see now
as it is. Before, we saw only ugliness, weaknesses, and
bad attachments. Now Jesus shows us, emerging from
all these shadows, our beauty, our strength, and our

edom. We sought ourselves. In finding Jesus, we have found our true personality.

We see Jesus bending over sinners with pity and delicacy. Would he have done so if our misery were incurable? He waits for them, he calls them, he gathers them, he pursues them, he moves them, he raises them up again, he changes them, he makes saints of them. Therefore, we never rebelled, we were only lost sheep. Nor is our nature powerless to do good. If it were, what would be the point of the reproaches that Jesus addresses to the Pharisees who have strayed from the path of virtue? Or why would he say to his disciples when they were slow in entering into his spirit, "You know not of what spirit you are"? (See Lk 9:55, footnote). You do not know all that you can do. If they were incapable of doing good, would he encourage them to be perfect? Instead of adhering to the letter of the old law, he wants the virtue of his people to surpass that of the scribes; he urges them unceasingly to advance more and more in the way of charity. The whole gospel is a solemn affirmation of the ever-growing capacities of human virtues.

Our strength does not consist in the vain estimation of our qualities and our merits, nor in any pretended capacity to bear pain and sorrow. "Whoever exalts himself will be humbled" (Mt 23:12). The really strong person is the one who lives in God, who implores his help and submits always to God's will. The secret of our power, of our capacity, is in our union with the Man-God who was given us. It is always the Spirit of Jesus which prays in us, which fights in us, which triumphs in us.

7

OUR NEED FOR GOD

The woman said to him, "Sir, you have nothing to draw with, and the well is deep; where do you get that living water? Are you greater than our father, Jacob, who gave us the well, and drank from it himself, and his sons, and his cattle?" Jesus said to her, "Every one who drinks of this water will thirst again, but whoever drinks of the water that I shall give him will never thirst; the water that I shall give him will become in him a spring of water welling up to eternal life." (John 4:11–14)

The most excellent gift can leave its recipient indifferent if its value is unknown. Jesus, having presented himself to the Samaritan woman as the gift offered by the eternal love of God, now proceeds to enlighten this soul, to make it conscious of its spiritual needs, to awaken in it a longing for divine things, and to inspire it with a desire for God.

He does it in allegorical terms, in which we will no longer find the direct and simple manner of the Synoptic

Gospels. Perhaps we can say that the language of St. John's Gospel is the best suited to an analysis of our interior life.

The first impression is that the woman has understood none of the things Jesus said to her of God's gift and of the living water she should seek. She is still at the stage of the *animalis homo* (unspiritual, or natural, man) of whom St. Paul speaks, who is not yet regenerated and who cannot understand things of the Spirit of God (1 Cor 2:14).

To her credit, we see a respectful attitude toward Jesus. She no longer addresses him as "You, a Jew." Now she calls him "Sir." This is not yet religious homage, but the title one gives to persons of note. When St. Mary Magdalene, on the Resurrection morning, thinks that Jesus is the gardener, she also calls him Sir. (Jn 20:15).

All the same, the rest of her reply shows that she hardly suspects the level to which the Savior has suddenly raised the conversation. All she knows is that this foreigner, who boasts that he can give her living water, has no vessel in which to draw it up, although the well is deep. Does this mean that he knows some hidden spring nearby? But what water can equal that given to us by our father Jacob? Or can this man be greater than Jacob? Maybe as powerful as Moses who drew water out of a rock?

It would be easy to presume an ironic intention in the woman's questions; but her embarrassment leads one to believe rather that she has some intuition of the superiority of the man who is talking to her. Her mistake is indeed excusable, for the expression that Jesus uses, "living water," was used by everyone to mean running water. Why should she have looked further for any other meaning?

The Gospel according to St. John gives us many examples of confusion that certain words used by Jesus caused in the minds of his hearers, and of their astonishment or outright protests. Jesus then does away with all the ambiguity by revealing the figurative meaning—mystical or spiritual—of words taken literally. For instance, he tells Nicodemus that in order to enter the Kingdom of God, one must be born again. The old doctor objects: How, at his age, could he be born a second time? The Savior then explains to him that he means a spiritual rebirth. (See Jn 3:1–21.)

In the same way, when our Lord first announces the Blessed Eucharist, the people of Capernaum think he is proposing some sort of cannibalistic rite: "How can this man give us his flesh to eat?" Many of them went away without having understood that his words are "spirit and life," that it was not their bodies which Jesus meant to feed but rather their souls, by communicating to them, in the sacrament of his body, an increase of divine life. (See Jn 6:22–59.)

In the same way, he says, "Our friend Lazarus has fallen asleep, but I go to awake him out of sleep." The disciples take him literally: "If he has fallen asleep, he will recover." This time Jesus tells them plainly: "Lazarus is dead." He wanted to teach them that our death is a sleep from which we shall awake unto the glory of God. (See Jn 11:11–15.) This way of speaking, so different from the parables, succeeds like the latter in fixing the attention of his audience on an image, which the Lord then uses to illustrate his teaching.

In the Samaritan woman's case, the ambiguity concerns the words "thirst" and "living water." She thinks only of the water she uses every day. But our hearts feel other thirsts that nothing on earth can quench. So Jesus offers us a mysterious living water—which theologians call sanctifying grace—and which will ease our torments.

This image was nothing new for the pious Israelites who sang in one of their psalms, "My soul thirsts for God, for the living God" (Ps 42:2), and the prophets had often urged Israel to drink at the springs of salvation. Jesus, in two other passages of the fourth Gospel, uses this image again: "He who believes in me shall never thirst" (Jn 6:35). And on the last day of the feast of Tabernacles, as the procession of pilgrims passed, escorting the priest who brought in a golden jug the water of the libations from the Pool of Siloam, the Master cried out: "If any one thirst, let him come to me and drink" (Jn 7:37).

Physical thirst corresponds to a periodic bodily need which a glass of water satisfies. But if we do not get that water, or if we have a fever, thirst can become unbearable. One can live many days without taking food; one cannot live more than three or four without drink.

In the same way, when the most profound needs of the human being remain unsatisfied, a moral thirst consumes us which, like the physical, can trouble our spirit and crush our will.

Shall we list all the desires of man, from the mo elementary to the most elevated? We would have to examine our whole life. We are thirsty for happiness, which begins—let us not be ashamed of it—with material conditions: security for tomorrow, independence, comfort, well-being, and riches. For we always desire more than we possess. At the same time, we need health, we need affection and trust. One sighs for rest, another is impatient for new activities. This one seeks distraction, another wants only silence. And while we ask for still more happiness from life, it seems to take pleasure in removing, one by one, those joys that it has loaned us.

This worldly satisfaction is only partial and temporary: our desires return immediately, and they return with increased strength. We want again, we want more, we want better. This life cheats our thirst: it cannot quench it. But, at the edge of the well, sits our Savior. He knows the cause of our too numerous and too vast desires, and he will satisfy them: "Whoever drinks of the water that I shall give him will never thirst." He will make this water gush forth from the bottom of our hearts: *Fiet in eo fons aquae salientis* (Will become in him a spring of water welling up; Jn 4:14). He relates the infinity of our desires to the infinite God who inspires them in us; and our life, united to God's, becomes eternal.

Let us grasp the symbols here. Jesus reveals us to ourselves. He solves the apparently insoluble contradiction between the immensity of our aspirations and the limits of our present condition. If the earth cannot satisfy all our desires, it is because we are made to go beyond the earth. The God who regulates our present life is the same God who created our soul. Our desires and limits coincide for a certain time, but then they must separate. At the best of times, they are not in harmony.

Our deep dissatisfaction here on earth is a proof of our greatness and a guarantee of our destiny. We are made for the Absolute.

"He who believes in me shall never thirst." "If any one thirst, let him come to me and drink!"—Lord, who has walked our roads from Bethlehem to Calvary, so as to experience our human thirsts, I come to you, I believe in you. *Da mihi hanc aquam* (Give me this water). Pour me out the draught of eternity.

8

WHAT GOOD IS RELIGION?

The woman said to him, "Sir, give me this water, that
I may not thirst, nor come here to draw." (John 4:15)

Our first reaction, on hearing this reply, could easily
be a gesture of impatience. Is that all that occurs
on hearing the Savior's teaching? Jesus has just taught
us wherein our greatness lies. He shows us how to read
into ourselves and see, in our infinite desires, the proof
of our divine origin. He assures us that the infinite that
torments us is a sign of our destiny. Better still, that here
below, God unites his own life to our human nature to
transform it into eternal life. And all the while, she is
thinking how useful not to have to come to this well anymore to draw water.

But can we be surprised that this woman, half pagan
and wholly a sinner, does not appreciate the symbol-
ism of the living water? Many baptized are completely
unaware of the greatness of their baptism and ignorant
of the obligations which flow from it. Have you never
been surprised by Christians who ask themselves, what

use is my religion? It is, in fact, of no use to them, and if they were to renounce their Christian faith tomorrow, their life would be in no way changed. Their religion is separate from their life. They have understood nothing about God's gift. They show a state of spirit much akin to the Samaritan woman.

It would be too much to presume that she misunderstood Jesus' thought completely. After asking him, "Where do you get that living water?" she has a feeling that it is not natural water, but comes from some place higher than this earth.

"You would have asked him, and he would have given you living water," Jesus had said to her. With docility, she then asks him for this supernatural gift, however obscurely she understands it. "Give me this water," she answers him, as later the Jews to whom he promised the bread of God said to him, "Lord, give us this bread always" (Jn 6:34). Neither she nor they really knew what it was they were asking, but if one were to know the full value of God's grace beforehand, who would have the audacity to ask for it?

Do you think that one would have to look very far to find people who, without expressing it in such a childish fashion, do not have a very much more exalted idea of religion? They look only for temporal advantages from it or regard it as a spiritual shortcut. Their piety is not so much worship of God as an indirect form of self-worship.

This is a tragic misunderstanding, the cause of great deception and revolt: What is the use of praying and practicing our religion if God still sends us trials? It's not worth my while going to confession or Holy Communion; I am no better or no worse for it. What is the use of religion? All this is the same thing as saying: "Sir, give me this water, that I may not thirst, nor come here to draw."

Nor come here to draw! Is the woman's request so strange after all? Like so many others, she wants her existence to be less hard and less monotonous. And many others, like her, expect from religion some consolation for the toils of life. Otherwise what good is it?

Certainly also, if obedience to the divine laws were to become the general rule, there would undoubtedly result a notable diminution in our sufferings and an increase in our well-being. For it is normal that what is good should produce happiness. Nevertheless, there is a great difference between this expectation and demanding that God should pay our wages from day to day and grant us a favor in return for every good deed we perform.

I prefer not to think that some Christians profess their religion only in order to draw temporal advantages from it, but how then could I explain their complaints against Providence when some trial strikes them while some wrong-doer is spared? The gospel is quite clear on this point. Our heavenly Father lets his sun shine on the wicked as well as the good. (See Mt 5:44–45.) Jesus has a very harsh answer for the man who begs him to defend his case in a dispute over an inheritance. He condemns avarice, cupidity, and even care for riches. (See Lk 12:13–21.) He promises us persecutions and struggles, but he has never promised health or fortune.

And is it not the contrary which ought to scandalize us? If virtue were to have its immediate reward, virtue would be good business, abstention from sin a profitable investment. It would be the end of all morality, in that we would pursue well-being and would no longer love the good. This is why Jesus wants us to rely in a filial way on our heavenly Father for all our earthly necessities, beginning with our daily bread. Let us add to his love the share of benefits and restrictions, of favors and sorrows, which his wisdom has in store for each one of us.

God is good when he lets us weep just as when he dries our tears. And the Christian's faith ought to be strong enough to ask for a miracle, but also to be able to forego one.

SOURCE OF PROGRESS

What is the Christian faith? It is not a source of *profit*, but a source of *progress.* The advantages of believing consist in a greater capacity for moral advancement. What good is religion? It makes us better. Then, Lord, when I receive the living water of grace, I will still have to return every day to draw water from the well, so will it be the same afterwards as before?

The woman of Samaria will return to draw water every day, but it will not be the same as before. Henceforth she shall go to the well, alert and joyful; and go back to her chores, singing. The worries of her household shall not make her gloomy anymore; they shall not even be enough for her. She will go to lend a helping hand to others, seeking no other reward than the joy of having been useful to them.

For the Lord is faithful to his promises. It is really true that God helps us in our work, that he sustains us in our difficulties, that he consoles us in our trials. But that does not imply, on the contrary, that we no longer have to work, to struggle, or to suffer. Our lot is still that of all other human beings. The difference is that instead of collapsing under our burden, united to Jesus Christ we have the strength to carry it. We accept our fate and our work; we believe in the fruitfulness of sacrifice. As St. Augustine says, "For, in the case of what is loved, either there is no labor, or the labor also is loved." *Ubi amatur, non laboratur; aut si laboratur, labor amatur.* This is the use and the good of religion.

Nor come here to draw! This illusion and, as a result, the disappointment felt by some Catholics, relates more often to spiritual ease that they think ought to be attached to the practice of religion, but which is not, in their experience, its normal consequence.

COOPERATION WITH GOD'S GIFTS

If the result of grace—this word means the presence in us of the divine life—were to exempt us from personal effort, then it would not be a gift. The divine assistance, which is grace, is not given to us in order to eliminate our effort, but to make us capable of more considerable efforts and, in this way, accomplish something that would be beyond our natural possibilities alone.

In a war, when the commander sends reinforcements to troops facing a stronger enemy, the arrival of
the reinforcements does not authorize the soldiers who
have withstood the first attack to fall back to the rear.
They must continue to fight. But helped by the reinforcements, they can counterattack. This is also what prayer
and the sacraments bring us. They do not dispense, they
strengthen.

Let us continue to learn from the gospel. The graces
of the Christian life are like the seed whose germination,
growth, and fruit depend on the different soils in which
it falls. The ground needs to be cleared, worked, and fer-
tilized. You have received the strength of Jesus Christ in
the Eucharist. He is united to you. But are you united to
him? What else have you done?

"I have received him. It is up to him to act," recalls
the servant in the parable who hid his talent so as not to
lose it, whereas his duty was to make it grow by his own
work. His master condemned him as wicked and lazy.
Without a doubt, he was lazy. But wicked? What wrong
did he do? He abandoned God's gift (See Mt 25:14–30).

How do we imitate this wicked and lazy servant?
How about when temptation overcomes us because we
did not pray? Do not expect that God will change the
nature he has given you, but he will undoubtedly help
you to improve. He helps us very much but he demands
solid effort on the part of our own free will.

What good is religion? It allows us to become better.
To become a child of God. One can grow physically and
remain merely a big child all one's life. One becomes an

adult only by a voluntary, courageous, prolonged, and often painful moral effort. In the same way, to become a child of God, all our energy, our patience, and our personal tenacity must cooperate with the free gifts and the innumerable helps that Christ gives us through his Church.

So it is still necessary—and always will be necessary—to go to the well for water: that is to say, we will always have to watch, to resist, to struggle. Every confession gives us more courage to accomplish sacrifices, which will convert us more. Sacramental absolution does not exempt us from making sacrifices. It inspires us to make new and harder ones. Each communion helps us to strip ourselves of our selfishness so as to become one with Jesus Christ. The Eucharist itself suppresses neither our selfishness nor the need for sacrifice. It makes us renounce self even more and makes us pursue our selfishness to its last strongholds. To pray is not just to sit back and wait to see what will happen. It is to enter boldly into the will of God and give ourselves up to it entirely.

"Have care for me," our Lord said to St. Catherine of Siena, "and I will have care for you." Let us not care for ourselves anymore. Let us entrust to him all the interests of our life, those of our soul and our eternal destiny, never again to attach ourselves to anything contrary to his glory, to his reign, to his will; this should be our only care.

Only Jesus can accomplish this marvel in us. For it is true that the beginning of religion is in us: our poverty, our restlessness, our need of happiness. But the moment we meet Jesus Christ our thirst for happiness is quenched, as he promised the Samaritan woman. Henceforth, we thirst only to please him and to resemble him.

We forget ourselves, entering into God's work. We give up the idea of using religion for our own ends; we make of it a service: service of God and service of God on earth in the person of our companions.

No more selfish calculations. The problem of our human progress and our own salvation is solved by the dual love of God and of our neighbor. We have tasted the living water which Jesus gave us to drink, and the love of ourselves has melted into charity.

9

THE KNOWLEDGE OF SIN

Jesus said to her, "Go, call your husband, and come here." The woman answered him, "I have no husband." Jesus said to her, "You are right in saying, 'I have no husband'; for you have had five husbands, and he whom you now have is not your husband; this you said truly." The woman said to him, "Sir, I perceive that you are a prophet." (John 4:16–19)

The divine truth is inaccessible to the spirit of man as long as he remains a prisoner of sin. The unbelievers who went to the French village of Ars, to consult the holy *curé* St. John Vianney on the difficulties which kept them outside the Faith were invariably told: "Begin by going to confession." When Bl. Charles de Foucauld presented himself to Abbé Henri Huvelin to ask him for instruction, he received the same reply: "Go on your knees; confess; you will believe." "But I have not come for that." "Confess!"[1] The future blessed hermit of the

---

1. René Bazin, *Charles de Foucauld: Explorer of Morocco, Hermit of the Sahara* (Paris: Librairie Plon, 1921).

Sahara knelt and all his doubts disappeared. This is the normal course taken by conversions.

"Confession! I am not ready for that yet," says the one still seeking the truth, but in vain. Yes, you are ready for that, you have reached the point where there is nothing more between yourself and God but the mists of sin. The very moment you accuse yourself of your sins, your eyes open to the light.

Only the pure of heart can see God, and Jesus is about to cut short the Samaritan woman's delays by making her take note of her sins. With what tact Jesus succeeds in winning over this sinner who has not yet gotten rid of her pride! He uses no severity, no reproach, and he carefully avoids humiliating her. He is satisfied with showing her that he is the master of her conscience.

She tries to parry Jesus' first question: "I am not married." That is true and not true. She is not lying, but trying to avoid the issue. However, in this lack of candor, Jesus does not see arrogance as much as sadness, nor does he reprimand her for her subterfuge. He pities her, and to spare her too painful a confession he lays her faults before her.

Many commentators would like to think that, before living in sin, the Samaritan woman had contracted five regular marriages. The difficulty here is that she would have had to have been a widow five times in succession, which is difficult to admit, or else that she had been divorced each time. Now, the causes for which the Mosaic law allowed the *libellus repudii* (or, broken contract) were not such as to make us sympathize with her if she were in fact put off. One inclines to think her unions were unlawful.

A little further on, in fact, we hear her say to the inhabitants of Sichar: "Come, see a man who told me all that I ever did." Jesus therefore did not show her only present sin, but also all those she had committed before. The past was probably no better than the present.

Faced with this unexpected revelation, she seems impressed above all by the character of the man who is able to read into her life, but the rest of the narrative leaves no doubt as to her repentance. It is as if she says, "Lord, you knew that! I see indeed that you are a prophet. What, Lord! You knew everything when I was approaching the well and you did not turn away from me! You knew how unworthy I was even when you were promising me the living water of salvation!" In turn, the Lord essentially tells her "I have not only promised, but also have given you the first drops of salvation by making you aware of your sin."

Perhaps we would be disposed more favorably toward her, if, like another sinful woman, she washed the Savior's feet with her tears, wiped them with her hair, and anointed him with oil. But, from the experience of converted sinners, we can well believe in her sorrow. When they accuse themselves for the first time, they still have not grasped the full gravity of what they're doing. They are only happy to feel the weight that was oppressing them fall away. It is only later, when sanctifying grace has enlightened them, that they understand their guilt better; then they deplore it with a bitterness that they did

st and they still weep for their faults long
forgiven them.

in this perspective that St. John narrates the
of the Samaritan woman. She could not see
anything as long as her sins blinded her. The moment
that she saw that she was guilty the light penetrated into
her soul.

The darkness symbolizes the spirit's blindness which
St. Augustine compares to a veil covering the eyes: the
eyes can see neither the objects surrounding them, nor
the veil which hides these objects from them. In the same
way, the sinner is in darkness and knows nothing of faith
or of spiritual values. He is equally insensible to the state
of sin which causes his moral blindness.

The sinner's blindness consists in not recognizing
his sinfulness. There are very many pretexts. He shelters
behind the "destiny" that governs actions (which does
not stop him from giving himself the credit for any good
he may do, nor from condemning those who do him
wrong); or else he asserts that to follow nature cannot be
wrong (as if the virtuous man were not doing honor to
human nature precisely by resisting his evil inclinations);
or again he persuades himself that what we call pride,
cupidity, and luxury, cannot offend God who is so much
above all our petty attacks (when, in fact, to infringe
against God's laws is nothing less than to usurp his place
in substituting his will for ours.)

The capital heresy of sinful humanity is the denial of
sin. If sin does not exist, what good is there in conquer-
ing one's instincts? And besides, what good is a victory

which makes one suffer? Progress has no meaning to the man who is satisfied with himself. He can only live for himself as best he can, ceasing to be interested in others when he has gotten enough use out of them.

Will we be satisfied with hoping that these senseless egotists may turn perhaps at the hour of death toward the God whom they have despised all their lives? Like the mole who lives underground and always keeps its eyes closed, but then, when it is about to die, comes out and sees the light for the last time?

Let us pray that Jesus' phrase may re-echo in their ears: *voca virum tuum* (Go, call your husband). Go and find your sin.

The sun will dissipate their darkness only if they first agree that they are living in darkness. They will be saved on the day when, like us and with us, they beat their breasts and say: *Peccavi!* (I have sinned!) One begins to leave sin behind when one confesses: I have done wrong. I have been unjust, I have fled from good. At that moment, the darkness turns to light and one can then add: I have offended God. For God makes himself known to whoever retracts his sin. From the moment we denounce ourselves, Jesus Christ forgives us.

ADVANCING TOWARD SANCTITY

Then Jesus suggests the right penances. He makes us desire virtue. He holds us up. If we fall again, he raises us up immediately, forgiving us once more because we repeat, I have sinned. We progress only under the condition that we never forget that we are sinners. The more we advance toward sanctity, the more acute becomes our sense of sin.

Now we come to some considerations, not for the sinner living in darkness, but for those who have grown up in the light. Ask yourself, is my faith really living? Is the gospel the great ideal that inspires my whole life? Is Jesus Christ my friend who never leaves me? If you cannot reply to these questions with a categorical "yes," then you are moving toward darkness. *Voca virum tuum* (Go, call your husband). Look out, your sense of sin has been weakened.

And if we have never hated the light, can we pretend that we have never been afraid of it? Is it not for fear of seeing too clearly that many Christians seldom, or too superficially, make an examination of conscience? Let us be faithful every night to this appointment between Christ and our heart.

One also turns away from the light when, uncertain of one's duty, one neglects to understand it, and so remains in a half-light, which favors half-measures and leads to complete sin. Do you keep close by you that book which can enlighten you? Do you open, I dare not say every day, but from time to time, the New Testament, or some spiritual book? You have no time? That sort of thing does not interest you? Take care, the night will envelop you soon.

Finally, do you make one voluntary sacrifice every day? I am not speaking of those annoyances which come to us from our neighbors or from circumstances of life. I have in mind a freely chosen action every day by which we fight one of our passions and which is an antidote against sin. This is the most effective means, not only of keeping from moral decadence, but also of overcoming the intellectual temptations that try to deprive us of the light.

If we do not fight to the end against our selfishness, we will inevitably stray from the truth or mistake our illusions for the truth. Daily mortification is a part of any serious moral discipline. It helps us to judge our interior dispositions. Thanks to such actions, we have the command of our will instead of being subject to the fickle influence of our feelings. We master ourselves.

A child whose easy-going parents have satisfied all his whims and left his desires uncontrolled, even if he be without vice and possessed of an excellent nature, is nonetheless inclined to become irreligious. Selfishness ends up either in the negation of God or in the deformation of religion. And that remains true for us adults. The darkness that hides God from our spirit rises from our feelings and our heart. It is there that we must keep watch.

Let us now ask the Lord, why not give the Samaritan woman her name, at least the name that an old Greek tradition gives her: Photina, daughter of light? Like her, we who hesitate to look frankly inside ourselves, should ask the Lord to show us clearly all the blemishes which hide the truth from us. If we do not deny them, he himself will wipe them out.

10

THE NEW WORSHIP

"Our fathers worshiped on this mountain, and you say that Jerusalem is the place where men ought to worship." Jesus said to her, "Woman, believe me, the hour is coming when neither on this mountain nor in Jerusalem will you worship the Father. You worship what you do not know; we worship what we know, for salvation is from the Jews." (John 4:20–22)

S t. John's Gospel contains many sentences whose conciseness could displease a hurried reader. Of the three verses just quoted, the last alone has given rise to so many and such diverse commentaries.

Without going into a detailed work of exegesis, try to learn from the Savior's words. In this passage, and in the two verses which follow, he sets out principles which are to regulate the worship of God from that point forward. The old rites are to lapse. Draw your attention once again to the excellence of the Savior's teaching methods. Bringing souls to the truth is such a difficult art. Let us not neglect any of the examples he gives us.

Some people find in the Samaritan woman's eagerness to indulge in a religious controversy a desire to have her revenge on the prophet who has convicted her of sin. To do so, I think, is to judge her very rashly. Can one not ask a question without being immediately suspected of wrong motives? Has she not the right to clarify a doubt? And whom, if not the Savior who has just pricked her conscience, should she ask for enlightenment?

Contrary to suspicion, this woman's question hints of a note of sadness. She feels that, from now on, she will do whatever he asks of her. And that is what is troubling her now.

Our fathers worshiped on this mountain, and with her hand, Photina points to Mount Gerizim on which the temple of Manassas had been built. Even after the Jewish high priest John Hyrcanus had destroyed it, the Samaritans had continued to come to this place to offer ritual sacrifices. It is there that all her people pray, there that they will come again at every feast. Would she now have to give up the cult of her race and go down among the Jews to pray at Jerusalem?

We must admire the way in which Jesus calms her uneasiness. One can expound a dogma or a doctrine and leave the hearer with a message of "You can take it or leave it." But if a person is not ready to receive it, is there not a danger of relapse into old errors?

Now the Master exercises the greatest delicacy in his dealings with the neophyte: *Woman, believe me.* What gentleness there is in those three words, as though to say, "Have confidence in me, I am only anxious for your good. Believe in him who purified your heart. Can you doubt that he is telling you the truth?" Then he proceeds step by step.

Who are right, the Jews or the Samaritans? He does not tell her at first. Why should he offend her pointlessly, since both worships will soon have to give way to a religion from which all differences shall be banished? He reassures her! The true worshipers of God will have to go neither to Mount Gerizim nor to Mount Zion. The convert's patriotic feelings are spared.

Having given her this satisfaction, Jesus can then let her know a more painful truth. These two forms of worship must, indeed, disappear but the new and universal worship is to come from the religion of Israel, which remained faithful to the divine revelation, while that of the Samaritans was corrupted by ignorance. The Gospel continues and completes the prophets that Samaria repudiated; and it is the Jews who will give the world its Savior.

We, too, should use Jesus' method to lead those people who confide in us gradually toward Catholic doctrine. In the beginning, let us propose to them only the points they are prepared to understand. This first acquiescence may then weaken their resistance to other points. In any case, the truth will thus appear to them less hard, and be accepted with less difficulty.

The woman's question begins like this: "*Our fathers worshiped*," and Jesus ends the first part of his reply: "*will you worship the Father*." The problem changes its appearance immediately. Religion is not a human tradition, it is homage rendered to God.

Jesus decries the decadence of racial religions and of national cults. All are equally the children of the same Father. Later on, he will restate this in more moving terms. He wants to unite all in one fold, under one shepherd. The temple at Jerusalem will give way just as the temple at Gerizim was overthrown. When St. John was writing his Gospel, twenty years had passed since the Lord's prophecy about Jerusalem had been fulfilled.

God's immensity is not to be enclosed in buildings made by human hands. There is no exclusive place where we must meet God; there are no fixed days or times when he grants us an audience. We must give thanks to him always and in all places.

Such is the universal Church which the Savior announces to the Samaritan woman. He summons to it all people of goodwill who call God their Father. For the old sacrifices, he substitutes the essential religious act of adoration, which rises from the human heart and can everywhere and always reach the loving heart of his Father in heaven.

Here it is no longer Photina who opens her eyes in astonishment. The Christian universe is, in fact, crowded with basilicas, churches and oratories. We also have our given days of prayer and penance. Liturgy regulates our religious rites down to their minutest detail. We go on pilgrimage to holy places such as Rome, Assisi, or Lourdes, and countless others around the world. Can it be said that we have mistaken the Master's intentions?

Now the surest interpreter of Jesus' thought is Jesus himself. Just like ourselves, he, too, performed the acts which help us to adore the Father. Like us, he went on his knees when praying, he withdrew to a quiet place.

When he instructs the Apostles on their future ministry, he orders them to baptize, which is to perform a rite (See Mt 28:19–20). He gives them the power to remit sins, thus instituting many intermediaries between the Father and his adorers (See Jn 20:23). He orders the Apostles to repeat the Eucharistic meal: "Do this in remembrance of me" (See Lk 22:19). He tells them to stay in Jerusalem because there, and nowhere else, will they receive the Holy Spirit (See Acts 1:4). When he leaves in his Ascension, his farewell salute is a ritual gesture: "Lifting up his hands, he blessed them" (See Lk 24:50).

So unless we are foolish enough to think that Jesus Christ contradicted himself, we will have to agree that the universal and interior worship which he wished to establish does not exclude vocal prayer, meetings, or external rites.

He did not condemn Gerizim, any more than he denounced Mount Zion, but he makes clear their secondary importance when compared to interior adoration. It is not the *place* but the *prayer* which unites him to God.

Poor Photina. She praises the fame of Gerizim and does not realize that she is living in sin. The processions and sacrifices in which she has taken part never opened her eyes to her conduct, just as the liturgies of the temple at Jerusalem do not sanctify any better the priests and lawyers who send Jesus to his death. Exterior manifestations of religion are in vain if our life is not religious.

The ancient religions had completely separated morality from worship. It was easier that way. Now, that separation is excusable among pagans, but the law of Moses was clearly opposed to it. That explains why Jesus accused the so-called "devout" of his time of being hypocrites. The Savior would no longer tolerate these abuses.

Although exterior worship may be only a deceptive façade for the sinful, it does not follow that it should be rejected on that account. It is legitimate insofar as it helps us to find God within ourselves. It is of value to us, not to God. We, in order to find him, need our churches and the edification of collective prayer, and even more so, penance and the Eucharist.

Disciples of Christ, let us never despise those who go up neither to Gerizim nor to Jerusalem. Full of compassion, let us beg the Father to reveal himself to those blind people who cry out to him from the bottom of their hearts. By all means, let us spread the truth throughout the world with all our power, but may our respect for the truth never stifle our charity. Let us hold out a fraternal hand to all those who do not realize that they are going astray when they follow the traditions of their fathers. If a person seeks God, professing a religion honestly and sincerely, ought we not accept that person as our brother or sister?

11

UNITY IN TRUTH

You worship what you do not know; we worship what we know, for salvation is from the Jews. (John 4:22)

Although considerate of the Samaritan woman's good faith, Jesus nevertheless does not hesitate to tell her that her worship is founded on error: "*You worship what you do not know.*"

God cannot turn his back on those who find themselves, through no fault of their own, outside the Catholic Church, but who turn to him with an upright and obedient heart. These people form part of the society of the just which theologians call the "invisible Church."

But it would be a mistake to suppose that in abolishing the old forms of worship, the Savior was advocating individualism in matters of religion. He proclaims the necessity for religious unity, but this cannot be at the expense of truth.

Now, on all who adore the Father, our Savior has most definitely imposed a doctrine, precepts, a rule of

prayer, and leaders who will provide for th
needs, that is to say, all the elements that
positive religion. Adoration in spirit does no
pendence either in regards to dogma or practice.

"You shall adore the Father." Surely, everything is
contained in that. *But we reach the Father only through
Jesus, and we know Jesus only through the Church.* Let us
recall briefly these two principles which propose, not a
vague individualism, but the law of religious unity and
the duty of the apostolate.

Religious unity can be founded on truth. Truth is
one. The mistake of all those who advocate an amalga-
mation of different religions is that they want to establish
an exterior union of verbal resemblances, whereas only
identity of doctrine can create real unity.

Religious unity will never be brought about by the
fusion of contradictory beliefs with their unequal moral
precepts. Jesus, who wishes to establish religious unity
among people, relates it expressly to the revelation of
the Old Testament: "Salvation is from the Jews." And
as the notion of the fatherhood of God is by no means
clear in the religion of Israel, Jesus is going to remove it
from the domain of "figures" or symbols, to present it
to us in its reality.

The Son delivered us from the condemnation which,
as a result of sin, weighed on our race. Redeemed man
can henceforth find favor with the Father. But he cannot
do this by himself. "No one comes to the Father, but by
me" (Jn 14:6). Can one hope for a more categorical or
more precise declaration? One can obey the Father only

if one obeys Jesus; one can love the Father only if one loves Jesus. We can adore the Father only if the Spirit of Jesus prays within us. Faith in Christ, in his works, in his whole doctrine, is the only route that leads to the Father.

On this condition, other people can also become the adopted children of God, with all the prerogatives that the true Son enjoys. But it is necessary, at the outset, that they become part of the divine race, that they be regenerated by the Spirit of Jesus, who is also the Spirit of the Father.

Undoubtedly, God is a Father to all people. Their faith or disbelief, their virtue or vice, do not alter God's immutable dispositions toward them. But in the doctrine of the gospel, God is more than a Father. He is *the* Father. Jesus does not say to the Samaritan woman, You shall adore a Father, however your thoughts conceive him. He says, "You shall adore *the* Father": the Father to whom the Son is substantially united, the Father to whom the Spirit unites us if we give the Son the full adhesion of our faith and will.

In short, adoration of the Father is not just a manner of speaking, that could be adopted indifferently by hundreds of different religions. To worship the Father implies acceptance of the whole Christian doctrine.

But here again, and perhaps even more so, we come up against the partisans of religious individualism who say: We accept Christianity but not the Catholic Church.

The truth is that just as we cannot come to the Father except through Jesus, in the same way we cannot find Jesus except through the Church.

This statement puts people on the defensive: "It is precisely because of the Church," they reply, "that so many of our contemporaries turn their back on Christ. They would willingly give their allegiance to the gospel, but they refuse to submit to those dogmatic formulas and innumerable prescriptions obviously added by men to Jesus' simple doctrine, so that it has been deformed completely by them."

Many works have been devoted to the refutation of these criticisms. One can give only an outline of this refutation in a few words.

First of all, without the Church, we would never have known the gospel. Who introduced us to the gospel? It was men to whom the Savior confided the task of reforming the world. They preached the doctrine of salvation and drew up the Church's first "catechisms," those Gospels which we never tire of reading.

We have only to dip a hand into the living water to take up the draught that suffices to quench our thirst. We would not have this water if some inexhaustible spring did not feed the well or the stream which provides it. Its source is the Church.

NO COMPROMISE

The Church has preserved Jesus Christ for us; she preserves him for us in his whole personality. Her teachers ensure that Christ's doctrine is not altered. In every generation, her saints offer new proofs of the divinity of Jesus. Those who have seen Christ from outside the

Church have never known all his aspects: they have deformed and distorted him.

Thanks to the Church's tranquil refusal to compromise, we know him as he is. The Church has never allowed the changing of a single word of the primitive text of the Gospel, even if this or that word lent itself to discussions and misunderstandings. "I and the Father are one," said Jesus, and later on he said, "The Father is greater than I." "A contradiction," those on the outside cry, "it must be either the one or the other." And the Church replies obstinately, "It is both one and the other." The experience of Jesus Christ that she gives us solves this contradiction, for we understand that he is, at the same time, one of us and infinitely above us.

It is not the Church, it is the dissenters who place themselves in opposition to the religious charter given at Jacob's well. What has been the result of the separation of so many sects from the apostolic Church down through the ages? Worse doctrinal confusion and a most regrettable frittering away of the spiritual strength of humanity. What is more, religious individualism and dividing the Christian Church has brought back what Jesus wanted to destroy: national churches and racial worship.

Let us not be intimidated, therefore, by the attacks of religious individualism. *We adore that which we know.* Our Church represents the faithful evolution of Christ's thought, preserving his commandments for us in their integrity, and in this way, she gives us the fullness of his life.

If other Christian denominations apply themselves to making the gospel known in pagan lands, can one blame the Catholic Church which preceded them all for intensifying her missionary action today? And why should we be surprised to see her proselytizing at the heart of our western society, the victim of schisms, heresies, and irreligion?

Like the Samaritan woman's divine instructor, the Church will show herself tirelessly receptive to all those who seek, to all those who are in error, to all those who sin. But also like him, she will never compromise with sin or with error itself. She works without respite for the religious unity of all human families; yet she will never hasten its coming if it means sacrificing one particle of that truth of which she is the guardian.

12

ADORATION IN SPIRIT AND IN TRUTH

Jesus said to her, ". . . But the hour is coming, and now is, when the true worshipers will worship the Father in spirit and truth, for such the Father seeks to worship him. God is spirit, and those who worship him must worship in spirit and truth." (John 4:23–24)

What a vivid realization of God's presence to see someone in the intense fervor of prayer, or by being one of a crowd that was singing its repentance and faith. Interior adoration can do without gestures and formula, but it may also need to express itself. Then it vivifies and transfigures the words and sentiments in external actions.

Though true worship of God must be personal, it would be false to conclude that individual piety is the only sincere form of religion. On the contrary, religious individualism is the open door to all errors, to all excesses, to all laxity. Each of us ought to adhere individually to the truth, but remember that the truth itself is objective. It does not depend on our personal opinion: it is Jesus Christ who has made it known to us. All the true worshipers whom the Father seeks must therefore share the same faith. Bound together by unity of belief, and united by the bond of charity, they find themselves (by force of circumstances just as much as by Christ's wish) grouped together in a Church, which maintains, directs, and reinforces it.

What then, within this framework of a social and external cult, is the exact and positive meaning of adoration in "spirit and in truth"?

In order to grasp the Savior's exact thought, instead of looking for the possible meanings of the words he uses, it would be better to juxtapose or at least to compare the new cult with those that it is replacing: the semi-superstitious cult on Mount Gerizim held up beside the proper worship in Jerusalem. It will be instantly understood that in Jesus' eyes, the sacrifices of the old forms of worship are only symbols of the *true sacrifice (in veritate)* that God expects from then on. For the material offerings that worshipers in the past had brought to the temples, Jesus substitutes a *spiritual gift (in spiritu).* He wants us to give ourselves; this is the offering that pleases God, an immaterial worship, a true sacrifice, by which we can adore God in a manner less unworthy of him and more worthy of us.

Considered with this in mind, the Savior's new legislation fits exactly into both the religious history of mankind and the development of revelation, for he came not to abolish them but to fulfill them (Mt 5:17).

Jesus explains to the Samaritan woman: "God is a spirit." He gives us material presents, which belong to him before they are ours. But there is something that is truly our own: in bringing a free creature into existence, God dispossesses himself momentarily of his sovereignty, for our benefit. Our spirit, our heart, and our will are absolutely ours. We can use them in conformity with or contrary to the divine precepts. What God expects of us is that we should consecrate freely to him what belongs to us as our own: ourselves, our personality. God, all spirit, wants all our heart.

This spiritual adoration is the only kind that cannot be a pretense, the only one that acknowledges our dependence on God. When we grant him a share of our time or of our riches, if we even give up some of our joys for his sake, we still keep all the rest for ourselves. We do not really give *ourselves* unless we have given our *hearts.* We adore God only if we love him.

It is ourselves that he wants: let us not try to offer him ransom or substitutes. If we reserve a part of ourselves from his authority, we adore him in words perhaps, but not in truth. Should he detect an unbrotherly thought in us, he has no use for our offering as long as we do not make peace with our brother. There is no true adoration if our spirit does not submit to him entirely.

The gospel rejects our claim to separate religion and life, as if we could adore God on Sunday, while on the other days we sacrifice to idols: to money, pride, sensuality. As if God could be our All while we are praying, and then mean nothing to us in our other daily occupations. For God, our prayer and our life are one.

In the new worship, there will be two victims: one to be offered, our Lord, Jesus Christ; the other to be sacrificed, and this will be the worshiper's own self.

The victim, once offered, is never withdrawn, but is consumed as a holocaust. So our heart can no longer be shared between God and Mammon. It is no longer only our psalms and our canticles, but our whole life of obedience which must be a perpetual praise of God's glory. Our *ex-votos* (a religious offering given in order to fulfill a vow) and our pilgrimages can proclaim our gratitude, but our life also must be a song of thanksgiving. Our almsgiving and our fasts definitely make up, to some extent, for our insubordination, but God demands a more personal expiation: that of an amended, mortified, and reformed life, a life that has been put right. We loved ourselves more than we loved God. Only when our egotism has been completely sacrificed shall justice be re-established.

So, our adoration lays hold of our soul and of our life. As St. Augustine observed, we were looking for a temple in which to pray and Jesus replied, neither at Gerizim, nor in Jerusalem: "Become God's temple yourself."

Jesus says something else that we cannot leave without comment: *"For such the Father seeks to worship him."* He seeks children who are detached from this world and who come to him not merely for food and shelter. He seeks children who hold out their hand not only to beg, but also to ask him to guide them. He seeks true children who love him and who try to please him.

For such the Father seeks to worship him. My God, how often have you passed near me and been disappointed to hear only the words of my prayer while my heart was far from you, or been hurt at seeing my conduct? Lord Jesus, make our life more united to yours, our sacrifice joined to that of your Cross, be such, so as to give your Father the joy of finding those adorers whom he is seeking!

13

THE MESSIAH'S WORK

The woman said to him, "I know that Messiah is coming (he who is called Christ); when he comes, he will show us all things." Jesus said to her, "I who speak to you am he." (John 4:25–26)

Our Lord made God's intentions known to the Samaritan woman: when all people, rising above differences of nationality and race, would together with one heart adore the Father in heaven.

The woman recognized in these words an echo of the hope long cherished by the children of Abraham. According to the divine promise, the monotheistic faith of the Jewish people would become the religion of all people. Photina believes in the coming of the Redeemer, she knows that the Messiah is about to appear. If all is not yet clear for her, the Messiah, when he comes, will explain everything. Jesus replies, "I who speak to you am he."

Some critics have contested the authenticity of these words because they are not in keeping with Jesus' usual attitude. Usually he is most careful to hide his messianic dignity. When Simon Peter, enlightened from on high, confesses at Caesarea: "You are the Christ, the Son of the living God," Jesus warns his disciples not only to guard the secret of his divine revelation but "to tell no one that he was the Christ" (See Mt 16:16–20).

Over the course of the previous few centuries, the Jews had misconstrued the meaning of the prophecies. They were expecting an earthly Messiah who would throw off the yoke of Rome and re-establish by force of arms the ancient kingship of Israel. Before claiming publicly that he was the Messiah on Palm Sunday, Jesus needed to clear up the misunderstanding that clouded his contemporaries' spirits. He had to restore, in all its original purity, the true figure and function of the Messiah promised by God to the chosen people.

But in the intimacy of private conversations, he did not maintain the same reserve. He could explain easily to simple souls who he was. And this is a very touching part of the narrative, to see the Lord sharing this confidence with a sinner who has just been converted. He is to repeat this often: the repentance of publicans and courtesans will merit entry into the kingdom of the children of God long before the superficial virtue of the Doctors and Pharisees. And it will always be simplicity of heart that allows us to reach God, who remains inaccessible to the subtleties of reasoners and the morally mediocre who believe that they have nothing with which to reproach themselves.

I who speak to you am he. These words end Jesus' conversation with the Samaritan. They complete her conversion.

She now becomes an apostle of the gospel. Generally speaking, Jesus' words do not make such a strong impression on the modern reader.

This is very understandable. For us, Jesus is more than the Man desired by ancient Israel: he is the Son of God made Man. The Incarnation is the dominant fact of the religious history of mankind and the permanent principle of our relations with God. Messianism, on the contrary, seems to belong to the past, to a past that is over and finished, completely foreign to us."

This is a mistake. In becoming man, the Son of God did not renounce his mission as Messiah. He merely gave it its true significance. And this mission is still oriented toward the future. We no longer expect the Messiah (that belongs to the past), but we are still waiting for the completion of his work. What is more, it is we Christians who have to complete it, to fulfill it, by our personal action. And this point merits our consideration.

One should not be surprised at the faltering of the first Christian generation. Completely dazzled by the presence of the Son of God on earth, they needed some time to get used to the idea of not seeing him any more. And besides, it was necessary that Christianity should first be able to collect itself and become a cohesive force before mixing with the world so as to transform it by holiness and sacrifice.

But then the disciples realized that the *messianic work had become the function of the Church*, that without ceasing to try and win heaven, they had to bring about heaven on earth. They knew that if the individual destiny of the

Christian is to leave the earth to go to heaven, the collective task of Christians is to make the earth a fit place for heaven, and to make heaven come down to earth, to speak like the seer of the Apocalypse. What conclusions must we draw?

The Messiah! The word means Christ, notes St. John. The Messiah does not therefore belong to the past. He fills the whole future, and it is by the thought of the future that he keeps our spirits in suspense. As long as he has not yet returned to judge the living and the dead, the universe will await the hour of his triumph, which centuries of Christianity must work out and prepare with a holy impatience.

Between the Savior's two comings, his work is entrusted to the Christians. Let us understand the full extent of our task: it is our job to bring about the religious unity of mankind, to fill the world with holiness, and to make happiness reign in it.

We would be forgetting our messianic role if we only considered heaven in relation to ourselves. It is not myself alone that Jesus came to save; he redeemed all mankind. He wants the salvation of all people. When St. Paul thought of his old co-religionists, his heart was torn with anguish; he would have agreed to be *anathema,* to be separated from Christ, so that his brethren, those of his race and blood, might be saved (Rom 9:3). Like him, we should desire heaven, not only for ourselves, but even more passionately for all people.

APOSTOLATE IS NOT OPTIONAL

As heirs of the Messiah, we should win heaven for all, and for that sake, conquer the earth for Jesus Christ. Heaven and earth are equally part of the Kingdom of God.

The apostolate is not an optional occupation, but a strict obligation for all Christians. If some people, obeying a more pressing inner call, take leave of their country in order to go and convert non-believers, others have not done everything they should by accompanying the missionaries with their prayers and sacrifices. All of us must sanctify the corner of the world in which God has placed us. For the future toward which we should always be looking is not only the Great Beyond, but also the earth itself.

So our messianic function is just that which the prophets announced. The Messiah's reign ought not only to bring holiness, but with it the happiness which flows from justice. "But seek first his kingdom and his righteousness" (Mt 6:33).

The social duty of Christians is no less strict than their apostolic duty. The Messiah charged the workers of the Kingdom to relieve the physical sufferings of their brethren, to allay their moral pains. Evangelical charity is for mankind a message of peace and joy, a ray from heaven which enlightens and gives a new spirit to our earth. It will be our eternal beatitude so long as we have practiced it here below already. Now, there are two ways to be charitable toward our brethren. The first consists in leaving to them what we no longer need. The second is voluntary deprivaton so that others will not suffer. The latter only is Christ's true charity.

If we are Christians, we are ahead of our time; we belong to the future. By virtue of our Christianity, we ought to be of heaven, of an earth that is already sanctified and made peaceful.

Let us live our gospel therefore, which is the law of a perfect world, on this earth that is so imperfect. On this earth, which we leave one after another, let us practice toward one another the charity which expresses the joy of heaven.

14

Do Not Be Shocked

Just then his disciples came. They marveled that he was talking with a woman, but none said, "What do you wish?" or, "Why are you talking with her?" (John 4:27)

The disciples' return interrupts the conversation between Jesus and the Samaritan woman. In mentioning the disciples' surprise, St. John passes abruptly from the Savior's grave religious teaching to more human considerations. He thus shows an essential gospel characteristic, that it instructs equally as much on elevated dogmas which unite us to God, as on the simple duties which bind men together. We have as great a need to know one as the other.

The apostles had not expected to find Jesus in conversation with a woman. Consider the times. The condition of the Jewish woman was certainly superior to that of other Eastern women; the Law commanded that she be respected, and the history of the Hebrew people surrounded with honor the names of the national heroines,

Deborah, Judith, and Esther. All the same, the place which the Jewish woman normally claimed was the domestic hearth. There, her husband and children could admire and praise the strong woman of the Book of Proverbs.

In fact, she did not take any part in public affairs, and even her position in religion put her in a state of inferiority in relation to man. No ritual ceremony accompanied her birth. If boys had to be brought to the Temple from the age of twelve onwards, there was no age fixed for girls, and women were not held to the performance of the religious rites that were obligatory for men.

In our Lord's time, the rabbis consistently refused to undertake the education of women. "It is better to burn the Law," they said, "than to give it to her: as much as to teach impiety." Why this ostracism? The famous leader, sage, and scholar, Hillel the Elder gave this rather enigmatic reason for it: "Women bring preconceived ideas with them."

The married woman never left her house unless wearing a veil. No man ever saluted her in public, not even her husband: it was even less permissible to speak to her. This being the case, when the disciples recognized Jesus from afar, chatting with Photina, they must naturally have been shocked. As they approached, they could identify to whom he was speaking, and their uneasiness grew. A woman! A Samaritan! A sinner! Jesus dared to defy three prejudices.

"They marveled," writes St. John. They supposed that the Master, during their absence, needed something or some information. They did not reproach him for holding this conversation that they found so unexpected; they preferred to be silent and not to understand, rather than utter a disapproving word. "But none said, 'What do you wish?' or, 'Why are you talking with her?'"

The disciples' astonishment would be enough to place this episode at the beginning of Jesus' ministry. For the Savior was not going to be slow in eliminating prejudices and his disciples would have many other causes for astonishment. He would gather together all those whom the wise men of Israel held in contempt: Samaritans, sinners, publicans, Roman soldiers, the poor, children, and women. He was to be the defender, sometimes daring, always generous, of all those little ones who came and believed in him.

More particularly, he would raise up again the dignity of woman by re-establishing the marriage laws in their original simplicity: "The two shall become one." Women would be among his most faithful disciples. It would be the women of Galilee who would help him, and the apostles, from their personal means. He would allow to come to his feet the women who wept for their sins and those who were eager for light. Women would anoint his head, weep at his martyrdom, watch over his agony, and lay him out in the tomb. They, before the men, would receive the first news of the Resurrection and the first greeting of the risen Christ. By that time, his companions on the journey through Samaria would long since have ceased to be astonished.

The disciples returning from Sichar were unable to stop themselves from feeling surprise, but they refrain from judging. His disciples did not know then all that we know about their Master. But they are quiet when they do not understand. Their modesty and their discretion should serve as an example.

Let us also suspend our judgment when we are astonished. Time, reflection, or perhaps light from on high, will allow us later on to appreciate what we don't understand in a more prudent and, doubtless, more accurate way.

If we refrain from judging, it does not mean it stems from a broadness of spirit that could welcome equally two contrary ideas. We must always look for the truth and neglect none of its aspects, but we should simply retain the elementary wisdom of not wanting to judge until after we have understood. As long as we are astonished, we have not yet completely understood.

Nemo tamen dixit. But none said. None of the disciples lets himself question the Savior. Here their discretion is a sign of trust. Recognizing that Jesus had freed himself from the common rules, they prefer to doubt their own opinion rather than their Master's perspicacity and merits.

Those who astonish us are likely to be the people whom we should be following. History teaches us that certain truths, today unquestioned, were formerly held to be errors—that all innovators, and among them the saints, encountered their contemporaries' distrust. This is the price paid by leaders and forward-thinking people. They see what most people do not even glimpse.

Acts 5:27–42 show the Sanhedrin meeting to judge St. Peter and the Apostles. Most favored finishing off the new sect by executing its leaders. One Pharisee stood against them, the rabbi Gamaliel. "So in the present case I tell you, keep away from these men and let them alone; for if this plan or this undertaking is of men, it will fail; but if it is of God, you will not be able to overthrow them. You might even be found opposing God!" (Acts 5:38–39).

Let us adopt this rule of wisdom. Above men, there is God; above Christians, the authority of the Church. Let us submit anew to the decrees of Providence and the decisions of our spiritual leaders. In that way we shall be sure of never offending against charity and of always spreading the truth.

15

GOD'S PARDON

So the woman left her water jar, and went away into the city, and said to the people, "Come, see a man who told me all that I ever did. Can this be the Christ?" They went out of the city and were coming to him. (John 4:28–30)

One experience where the action of invisible grace can be best observed is in the conscience of the sinner who has just received divine pardon. What happens there upsets all preconceived ideas.

Take the example of the Prodigal Son. (See Lk 15:11–32.) While retracing his footsteps along the road to his father's house, he can't imagine the welcome that he will get. Such are his feelings of unworthiness that he has a statement prepared. He will ask his father not to consider him as a son any more, but to take him back among his hired field workers.

Is this not, in fact, the only thought that can occur to a guilty man before the person whom he has offended? Human pardons, however generous and sincere, do not succeed in chasing away all the shadows.

The divine forgiveness is completely different. The father in the parable does not agree that the repentant son should suffer a downfall, even if this would satisfy his own desire to make reparation. It is not enough to say that the prodigal son remains his son. He has become so all over again, and that is why he is dearer to him than ever. "To make perfect" is more than "to make." Similarly, "to forgive" means "to give still more," to give more than could be expected.

Only God can stretch mercy to this scarcely conceivable degree. However, there is something more marvelous still, and that is the change which God's forgiveness brings about in the soul of the absolved sinner. Once he is forgiven, the prodigal son does not even dream of going back to join the hirelings. He puts on the festive garments, the ring, and the shoes that the servants bring him. He sits down at the banquet arranged by his father as if he had never left home. He becomes again, completely and naturally, the son.

We should examine in more detail the tremendous change produced in a human heart by God's pardon. The Samaritan woman is one striking example that we can all apply to our own lives. It should inspire us with a greater appreciation of the divine mercy and a more lively gratitude to the Father who has to forgive us so many things.

God's forgiveness is a new creation which does not destroy a person's nature. His forgiveness wipes out the offense and cancels the eternal punishment that the sinner has merited. This forgiveness completely changes the sinner's frame of mind and will with regard to the divine law. Most remarkable is the rapidity of this change. At the very moment when God forgives, the sinner becomes another person.

Who would recognize in the converted Photina the same careless creature who approached the well, who replied so arrogantly, who argued so obstinately that she would, no doubt, have discouraged anyone else but Jesus? Now she is hurrying toward the town of Sichar, a messenger of Christ, a messenger of salvation.

Reliquit hydriam. She left her water jar. Was it full or was it empty? We do not know. She does not know herself. She has forgotten why she came. Her life has been completely altered. She leaves her water jar, as St. James and St. John leave their nets, to follow Jesus. One always has to leave something when one is setting out on the full Christian life. Conversion turns one upside down; in the winking of an eye, the past has gone; another existence has begun.

She left her water jar. This may also be to assure the Savior that she will return immediately, when he will have been able to allay the stupefaction of his disciples, and when she, for her part, shall have recruited some new believers. Jesus has not ordered her to go and inform her neighbors. It is she who is overcome by the need to tell others the truth that she knows and the enthusiasm which carries her.

Venit in civitatem. She runs straight to the town. She does not visit her own house. It is to the whole world that she wants to cry out that God has freed her from her misery, that she is no longer herself, that she is someone else, and that Jesus has wrought this miracle.

She does not return home. The Savior did not tell her, but she understood within herself that in order to follow him, one ought not even take the time to take leave of those at home (Lk 9:61).

If she had gone home to tell what had happened to her, she would not have been understood, her exaltation would have been mocked, people would not have wanted to believe that she had decided to change her life. Or rather, she would have been implored to give up such a mad course. The poor man will learn at the same time as the others that his Photina has become a creature of light. And even if she had been capable of making him join in her repentance, this would not have been enough to repay to God her debt of conversion. She must bring the whole town to Jesus.

This is not always understood. It is not unusual to hear the tempestuous zeal of converts being criticized. Their critics seem to think that they are ill-qualified to instruct others, and that a little more modesty would not do them any harm. These criticisms would fall to pieces immediately if people realized the transformation that grace works in the hearts of sinners, and how the love of God makes the memory, the thought of, the desire for evil, intolerable to them. God's forgiveness keeps them humble, which makes their conversion so unshakable.

Come, see a man who told me all that I ever did. Can this be the Christ? We should not make any mistake about the meaning of this statement, "Can this be the Christ?"

The Samaritan woman is not in doubt about it, but she does not forget what she was. She will never forget it. How could she set herself up as an evangelist? If she had affirmed something, she would have found plenty of people to contradict her. If she had said, "I know who is the Messiah," those who remembered what she had been would have shrugged her off.

She asks them only to come and see him! *Come*, only to hear him. Decide for yourselves. And in order to make up their minds, she confesses the only thing that could convince them. Bravely, she exposes herself to their scorn. She who, only the day before, would have put anyone who attempted to reproach her for her conduct sharply in his place, essentially says to them, "Come and see a man who has told me all that I was, a stranger who knew my whole guilty life. He has told me everything I have done, and he has not spurned me."

What lack of modesty could one find in this admission? She does not add—and this proves her humility—that her heart is purified from now on, that her irregular conduct is over. She does not say, "Come and see the man who has converted me." True converts stay convinced that they are sinners. She says to those people, who perhaps are jeering at her, or who are hesitant about following such a messenger, "Come and see a man who has revealed all my sins to me."

And just as he is the only one to give confidence to sinners who repent, so he is the only one capable of giving them the necessary courage to recover. We need someone to say to us, "It is hard, it is very hard to climb back up the slope, but you will be able to surmount the difficulty."

Jesus holds this sincere and comforting language for us. Though God no longer sees our sins, he cannot prevent sin from leaving blemishes in our nature that incline us toward evil: flights of fancy, sudden awakenings of sensuality, distressing weaknesses of the will. But with Jesus, recovery is always possible.

Perhaps recovery will be affected by sad relapses. These will sharpen the regret of the weakening convert, will inspire a more ardent prayer in him, and will make him understand, in the end, that he shall not be truly converted until he resolves to make the sacrifices that are right to free him finally from sin. On that day, the convert will know that in order to save himself, he must, like the Samaritan woman, seek to save others, not by means of edifying discourses or even by some virtuous actions, but by consecrating himself to the kingdom of God. Just as the Samaritan woman does not flee out into the desert, but goes to find her fellow townsfolk—all witnesses of her sin—and mixes with their way of life in order to lead them to Christ, so the convert experiences the fascination of this desire: to lead all to Christ.

16

CONFESSION OF OUR SINS

All that I ever did. (John 4:29)

Omnia quaecumque feci. (All that I ever did.) The shame that these words must have meant for the Samaritan woman has disappeared and given way to the sweetest humility. However numerous and grave her faults, she no longer feels their weight. The Savior who has made her realize their malice has discharged her from them. *All that I ever did!* These words that should only be pronounced with lowered head and in a soft voice, are now a cry of the action of grace. So Photina repeats them to everyone who comes along, fearlessly and without calculation. She cannot keep them to herself because she is being ruled by a new feeling: the love of God overflowing from a forgiven heart.

I would like to say something about confession, the discipline of the Church which has been most discredited. But one has only to show it in its true light in order to demonstrate all its benefits.

Only our Lord Jesus Christ could have thought of this method of calming the repentant sinner. Confession bears the marks of the Man-God, for it satisfies man's nature and God's rights at the same time.

Every guilty person feels the need to confide in someone in order to justify himself. But "justify" can be taken in a double meaning. The perverse wish to justify their misdeed to someone as tainted as themselves, while the pure of heart, the humble, and the converted who fall into a blameworthy action will go to confide in someone better than themselves.

The sinners who repent need to rehabilitate themselves. The excuses that they could make for themselves, the promises of expiation that they could make to themselves are not enough for them. They need someone to hear them, to judge them, to reassure them, to encourage them.

Some people will say: "What God asks for is repentance. Then what good is it to confess to a priest, to a mere man?" But by what sign shall we know that our repentance has really earned us God's absolution? This is why Jesus brought the forgiveness of heaven to earth and left it there. He charged his apostles with being the ministers of this forgiveness by giving them the power to remit or to retain sins, under a special influence of the Holy Spirit (Jn 20:22–23) and according to the rule of the gospel. The sacramental minister absolves the sins of his brethren, without having the right to forgive his own to himself. If he does not perceive a true repentance, he will apply himself to awakening it and invigorating it. He will only show himself immovable to pride or to scandal. Faults, however grave or numerous, can always be wiped out from the moment that the sinner 1) humbly regrets them, 2) determines to make reparation for them, and 3) sincerely wishes not to fall into them anymore.

These three conditions refute the criticisms that are leveled against Catholic confession under the pretext that, in facilitating forgiveness, it indirectly favors sin.

If it were too strict, the sacrament of penance would put the sinner off; if it were too easy, it would encourage relapses. Also, while taking our weakness fully into account, it maintains God's laws. Confession is beneficial exactly because it is difficult for our nature, and the pain necessary to compensate for the injustice of sin is precisely the obligation to tell everything that we have done.

All that I ever did. God asks us to recant our sins; now there can only be a recantation at the price of a complete confession. But a confession implies a confidant: a visible confidant who listens, who can ask questions, who sometimes reassures us and sometimes reproves us. Let us look at ourselves as we are. In the silence of one's conscience, it is easy to accuse oneself of all sorts of crimes. It is harder to accuse oneself of having committed an indelicacy or an injustice in front of a man. Yet, by this admission, we make reparation for our sins and raise ourselves up again.

Every sin also includes cowardice. One has retreated before a duty, given in before a threat, a smile, or to a stronger opinion. One has denied one's convictions or one's ideals. Confession forces us to take our courage in both hands. In that way, it makes up for our relapses or our mean actions.

PROOF OF REGRET

The detailed and accurate admission of sin re-establishes justice and represents a return to duty, an implicit promise to obey God. Rather than confession making one forget one's repentance, on the contrary, it leads to it. This proof of regret earns us God's forgiveness.

How should we make use of the sacrament of penance?

First, God alone is the master of his forgiveness. In giving us the means of salvation which our Lord entrusted to his Church, he has not restricted his power. He can therefore forgive outside of sacramental confession and, likewise, he can refuse to ratify the absolution of sin.

Second, every confession ought to be a new light and force in our life, but that depends entirely on us: Unless our personal effort corresponds to the divine, the sacrament does not produce this result and does not protect us against the harmful return visits of evil. And even if we have only venial faults to submit in confession, the rule is still the same: a total recantation by an exact confession.

Now many of these devotional confessions are so impersonal! People accuse themselves of defects that are the common background of human nature when they should be speaking of personal faults. The useful confession is the one in that one accuses oneself of perhaps only one fault, but one which has been really committed:

the humiliating shortcoming, the wicked premeditation, the hardness of heart toward a brother, or indifference as regards God.

Jesus certainly did not relate to the Samaritan woman all the defects of her life: he drew her attention to her guilty life. Confession is an interior survey which ought to awake contrition in us. A general view is enough here, provided it be sincere. It can happen that having rid themselves of grave sin, some people are worried that they will be reduced to accusing themselves always of the same sins in confession.

Let them trace from one confession to another an effort of amendment on some particular point, but not be discouraged because they regularly fall victim to the same weaknesses. Perfection is a drawn-out business.

However, it is useful to repeat the same things in confession. This proves that you are not resigned to mediocrity, and that you are continuing to struggle against your selfishness or slackness. This perseverance constitutes in itself a certain progress, as it would be a step backward to no longer regret your weaknesses.

Finally, frequent confessions that seem identical with one another are valuable in increasing in us the love of our Lord Jesus Christ. Doubtless, this is due to the sadness we feel at not having given better proof of our faithfulness. But instead of perpetually looking at our misery, we decide once and for all to see only God's goodness. We stop paying attention to the little that we do for him in order to consider all that he does for us. In this way, we realize our inability to raise ourselves. It is he who raises us up.

17

OUR REASON FOR LIVING

Meanwhile the disciples besought him, saying, "Rabbi, eat." But he said to them, "I have food to eat of which you do not know." So the disciples said to one another, "Has any one brought him food?" Jesus said to them, "My food is to do the will of him who sent me, and to accomplish his work." (John 4:31–34)

Ohn their return from Sichar, the disciples show Jesus the food that they had brought with them. He does not seem to be paying it any attention. An hour ago, he was worn out and thirsty. Now nothing tempts him. "*Rabbi, manduca.*" Master, have something.

No doubt the disciples have begun to help themselves in the hope that their example will entice him to join them, but then they stop eating. A guest who does not touch anything ruins the appetite of his fellow diners. Is their Master so tired that he cannot make the effort to feed himself? But with only half the day over, they will shortly have to set off again. They have a long walk before they reach their next stop. It is unreasonable. "Master, no matter how little, you must eat something. *Rabbi, manduca.*"

"I have food to eat of which you do not know." and his gaze is lost in the distance where he follows the hurrying steps of the converted sinner. In the distance, he sees the people of Sichar who are getting ready to come and find him. The disciples feel he is so far removed from them that they give up trying to make him explain his enigmatic reply. They ask each other for an explanation.

A food of which you do not know! St. John's Gospel often recounts the Savior's mysterious statements that use earthly terms to signify spiritual realities. Such was the living water that Jesus offered the Samaritan woman. This unknown food must be the same thing, something the disciples cannot grasp.

Their glances fall on Photina's water jar. Has she given him a drink or a piece of bread? Then Jesus cuts short the arguments by which they are going astray, "My food is to do the will of him who sent me, and to accomplish his work."

How hard we find it to answer if asked what we are doing with our lives. We are living, that is all. We are at the mercy of events. And on the other hand, we possess the power of using those events, sometimes for our good, but often in order to make our life a little more miserable. A mistake in the choice of a career, an error in conduct, some blunder, or just plain bad luck, and the result is disaster, irreparable sufferings for us and our descendants. "One's whole life," noted the French writer,

Augustin Cochin "depends on two or three *yes's* and two or three *no's*."[1]

PRINCIPLE OF UNITY

Rather than actions or experiences that take place in life, a principle of unity is the reason for living. Everything becomes clear, everything is acceptable, everything is beneficial in our lives, if our reason for living is the same one as that which made Jesus forget food and drink, tiredness and rest, the lateness or the urgency of the hour. *My food is to do the will of him who sent me, and to accomplish his work.*

Who sent me. *Qui misit me.* God entrusts a *mission* to us. We have to find out the intentions of him who has sent us, both his general intentions for the whole human race and also his particular intentions for each one of us. Then we ought to want these things and to do our best to achieve them.

God has sent us to labor at his work or, as Jesus puts it, to *accomplish his work.* His work and our work are one and the same thing. If we ourselves were the object of our life, our life would be without an object. Its object includes and goes beyond us.

This is our daily task. It consists in making the beauty that results from order and all the happiness which our love can inspire, reign, first of all in our own home—but

---

1. Augustin Cochin, *Les Espérances Chrétiennes* (Paris: E. Plon, Nourrit et Cie, 1883), 258.

also around it, in all the spheres of ordinary human activity. Our daily task, even in our most humble occupations, is not only our personal affair, it is the Creator's work, which we are called upon to continue.

Our reason for living is to perfect the work of him who has sent us: to perfect it first in ourselves, to perfect our personal creation by realizing more and more our status as sons of God; then to perfect it around us by spreading the kingdom of God among all people. Do not see these two tasks as alien to your profession or to your civil duties. They are part of your work, which is the work of God. We sanctify ourselves and we sanctify the world by transfiguring our daily actions and our relations with others through the love of God. In earning our bread, we earn heaven for ourselves. In selling good merchandise to others, in being good to all, we communicate to them a little of our Christianity. Our whole life is a divine work, once we do the will of him who has sent us.

18

CHRISTIAN OBEDIENCE

Jesus said to them, "My food is to do the will of him who sent me." (John 4:34)

Our Lord's words throw a light on the meaning and grandeur of our present task. Like Jesus, we are on earth to do the will of him who has sent us. If only we could say, like him, that to accomplish this is more necessary to us than our indispensable daily bread!

It's an unexpected comparison, but still a quite accurate comparison. We can only live on the condition that we feed ourselves: food gives to the living being the strength to live. Such is, in Jesus' eyes, obedience to the will of his Father: it is his reason for living, it is also *the strength of his life.* Let us make an attempt to share this Savior's conviction.

The Letter to the Hebrews teaches that "Although he was a Son, he learned obedience through what he suffered" (Heb 5:8).

Didicit obedientiam! He learned obedience: what an apprenticeship! St. Paul sees in it the depths of Jesus' humiliation. "He humbled himself and became obedient unto death, even death on a cross" (Phil 2:8). At Gethsemane, his obedience reaches its culmination when he renounces his own wishes in order to accept the order which sends him to his death: "Father . . . not my will, but thine, be done" (Lk 22:42).

The Savior's example moves us; but it does not reconcile us infallibly with obedience. Obedience always implies the sacrifice of our will, and this explains sufficiently why man does not like to obey. To obey is always *to surrender*.

Again, if God were giving us orders directly, we would perhaps submit with less difficulty, but we have to obey people who exercise his authority with respect to us. "He who does not love his brother whom he has seen, cannot love God whom he has not seen" (1 Jn 4:20). How shall we obey God whom we do not see, if we refuse to obey a man whom we see and who gives us orders in God's name?

Whatever he does, man is obeying. He surrenders to someone or something. Ordinary speech proves it. The person we admire respects the laws of honor and makes his pride the servant of his duty. The peaceful citizen submits to the country's laws, the worldly man to the customs of society. To brave the judgment and laws of men, one has to run counter to the forces that make us surrender.

A HIGHER PLANE

But the gospel puts us on a higher plane, where to obey is no longer merely to act in a reasonable manner by submitting ourselves to a legitimate and wise authority. It is no longer a question of surrendering. To obey is to want what God wants. *Non mea voluntas, sed tua.* Not my will, but thine. Obedience has gone beyond the will that limits itself to carrying out orders. Obedience penetrates the spirit. It inspires the judgment that our reason transmits to the will.

Simple obedience in conduct is, of course, not without merit, but it can be that of the automaton who servilely performs an order without questioning it, or the mercenary who is waiting for his wages.

Christian obedience makes God's law our interior law. It unifies our desires. It identifies what I should do with what pleases me. From that moment on, our liberty is no longer checked by any contrary desire. Instead of our will being immobilized by the opposing play of two antagonistic forces—God's and mine—they act in the same direction. Our possibility of doing good is reinforced by our desire to do it.

The gospel has worked this revolution among men. Until then, man only knew the law decreed on Sinai amidst the terrible flashes of lightning, the law engraved on tablets of stone to which one submitted under pain of death. Jesus engraves his law on our hearts, where that law is a source of light and of life. No longer by fear does he impose himself on us, but by teaching us God's love.

Listen to our Savior when, obedient unto death on the cross, he gives himself up to his torture: "I do as the Father has commanded me, so that the world may know that I love the Father. Rise, let us go hence" (Jn 14:31). It is the same filial and loving obedience which he expects from us: "If you love me, you will keep my commandments" (Jn 14:15). The law is no longer a constraint. Obedience is henceforth only a proof of affection, and one of three ways we offer him our freedom.

First, in order to escape the tyranny of the instincts to become more free, we may not turn our nose up at the moral laws. On the contrary, we will become ever more the master of ourselves by trying to know our own feelings better, by trying to understand the Legislator's intentions and by putting them into practice. No freer being exists than a Christian who obeys. By obeying, we become master of ourselves.

Second, obedience makes us capable of daring and bearing everything. The will of God presents itself to us in two ways: as a command to be carried out, or as a sovereign decision to which we should bow. In both cases, we find our strength by raising ourselves up as high as God's thoughts.

I have the strength to obey because I have elevated myself to the thinking of God, who loves his people. But to obey is not just to carry out an order. It is also to accept a plan of God's which is painful for us, such as mourning, adversity, or illness. We also, like Jesus, have to learn obedience by our suffering. In suffering, heroic sacrifice is accomplished whether we like it or not. We can only submit. Now, can this really be said to be obeying? It is the last word in obedience. It is not only to perform an act, but to accept a decision taken for us by our Father in heaven, and to make it our own.

Third, perfect obedience not only makes us abandon ourselves to God, it makes God live in us. The union between God and ourselves is so complete that the Savior cannot do better than to compare it to the assimilation of a food into our own being.

Similarly, when we obey another, our personality gives way to that other. If we love the person whose will we are doing, our intimacy is strengthened. Likewise when we fulfill the will of God, we make him live in us. Every act of obedience feeds the divine life in our soul, whereas our rebellions lessen his action over us and can go as far as killing our supernatural life.

Obedience is therefore a true sacrament, a real communion. "Our Lord," writes St. Vincent de Paul, "is in perpetual spiritual communion with the soul that does his will."

Is this not what Jesus pointed out in another case? His family, worried about him, had come to find him. People said to him, "Your mother and brethren are standing outside, asking to speak with you." And the Savior stretched out his hand toward the disciples by way of reply: "Here are my mother and my brethren! For whoever does the will of my Father in heaven is my brother, and sister, and mother" (Mt 12:49–50).

Let us stop at this adorable promise of our Lord's. He does not say to us simply that we shall have the place of the Blessed Virgin Mary and his kin in his affection. A real relationship created by the divine life makes of us his brothers, his sisters, and his mother.

19

CHRISTIAN OPTIMISM

Do you not say, "There are yet four months, then comes the harvest"? Behold, I tell you, lift up your eyes, and see how the fields are already white for harvest. (John 4:35)

When Jesus sends the seventy-two disciples off to proclaim the Kingdom of God, he shows them souls eager for the divine word as an already ripe harvest without enough workers. Our Lord alludes to a rural proverb that was familiar to the farmers of Palestine: "Between the sowing and the harvest, there are four good months." This translates to mean, it is useless to harvest before the four months are up; the crops need time to ripen.

But it does not take such a short time for the harvest of souls to come to maturity. Very often, much more time is needed, and sometimes much less.

A short time before, a sinner approached the well, wishing only to quench her physical thirst. But she received the gift of God. She became aware of her sins.

Her spirit was opened to the truth. In a few moments the seed sprouted, sprang up and ripened.

With purified soul and refreshed heart, this woman returned to her town and announced her joy at finding her Savior: "Come, see a man who told me all that I ever did. Can this be the Christ?" Seized with astonishment, her fellow citizens followed the humble and courageous neophyte; they came out of the city after her.

As Jesus is speaking to the disciples of this spiritual harvest, a group advances toward the divine Harvester. The seed thrown by Photina into these hearts is already springing up.

The Savior then explains the mysterious laws of the apostolate to those who are to continue his work. Before listening to this teaching, let us pause at the lesson of optimism and trust which Jesus wishes to give us.

The disciples are observing, in fact, but do not understand. Not an hour before, they were walking through the streets of Sichar looking for provisions. People had stared rudely at them with a suspicious air. The Apostles did not feel at ease either among these enemies of their nation and religion. And now, these half-pagan Samaritans are flocking toward Jesus.

Apostles in the World

The disciples had only exchanged a few words with the inhabitants to get their provisions and pay for them. It never occurred to them to reveal their identity, to confide in these foreigners that they had found the Messiah.

They left unsaid the good news already being preached. They did not speak of their lives, which had been transfigured by the Master's call and doctrine. Frankly, it had not occurred to them. Besides, how would their teaching have been accepted?

What the chosen disciples, the Savior's friends— Peter, Andrew, Philip, Nathaniel—had not done, a woman courageously did. What they had kept secret, this one-hour convert could not keep to herself. What is more, instead of the indifference, jeers, or hostility which the disciples may have feared, the inhabitants of Sichar had responded enthusiastically to Jesus through the words of a sinner. Won over by her enthusiasm, the whole village came in a mass before Jesus.

Lift your eyes and see. People are less evil, less far from the gospel than the faithful think. We come and go among them without dreaming of communicating something of our Christianity to them, or without daring to do so. Might they not need just this act of spiritual charity in order to come to Christ? Does it not also happen that Christians by birth are more timid than converts? And that humble people, those who have not studied, exceed others in the apostolate, the work of outreach and ministry?

Lift your eyes and see. Jesus also repeats to us this order of trust. Our faith is too bookish, it is too dependent on texts, it does not rely on him sufficiently. This is what makes us hesitant. Because we do not believe enough in him, we doubt others too much and we doubt ourselves too much.

See how the fields are white for harvest. The Gospel's severity against sin and the discipline which it imposes make people forget the optimism in Christ's message. The Christian ought to know how to suffer persecution for the sake of justice, how to weep with those who are weeping, and how to give his life for his friends. The Christian optimist does not cut himself off from realities, however miserable and sad those realities may be.

Christian optimism keeps and diffuses its calm: it is a social force. Even when events dash its hopes, it remains confident. It knows that the work of the good is never destroyed. It knows that the sacrifice is never in vain, and that, like its crucified Master, it is certain of victory. How can one believe in God and at the same time cherish despair in one's heart? God does not need four months in order to ripen the harvest of souls, to change evil into good, to make good the destruction wrought by sin, to save nations, to overcome tyrants.

However, he does need us. He demands of us trusting prayer and courageous action. He must have apostles in the middle of the world in order to spread the light of the gospel in the world. These apostles are parents in the home, the college student, the technician, and the office worker. Any Christian who speaks, reads, or writes, who radiates joy and inspires love for the truth, makes Jesus Christ loved by always being just and good. No other way converts the world, and this one will re-establish peace among men and lead them back to God.

20

SOWERS AND REAPERS

He who reaps receives wages, and gathers fruit for eternal life, so that sower and reaper may rejoice together. For here the saying holds true, "One sows and another reaps." I sent you to reap that for which you did not labor; others have labored, and you have entered into their labor. (John 4:36–38)

L
ed by Photina, the people of Sichar make their way toward Jacob's well. Within two days the little village shall be won over to the gospel. Jesus expresses the joy that his disciples will feel at the spectacle of this wholesale conversion, but, at the same time, he warns them against the illusion of a success too easily won. They should know, therefore, that other people, first Moses and the prophets, then many just men, and finally, this irresistible new-found convert, have prepared this harvest.

In order to produce a harvest, the seed must first be sown. Some, in their turn, will very often sow and not reap themselves. The proverb, "one man sows, and another reaps," is indeed true. When he is binding the sheaves, he ought not forget that another has cleared and sown the soil. And the sower, who will no longer be there when the crops are gathered into the barns, should not be sad at having worked in vain.

If this teaching of the Savior's concerns those who have charge of souls—parents, teachers, priests—it also applies to all Christians. Our Lord does not want us to be discouraged by the slow or slight results of our efforts which might make us believe that we have worked for nothing. But if our efforts are crowned with success, let us beware of giving the credit to ourselves. As Christ's representatives among souls, let us be both very patient and very humble.

Just as there are principles and methods of education, there are rules for the apostolate: nevertheless their influence is extremely variable and uncertain. Once we try to influence another either spiritually or morally, we must take into account free will, that person's inclinations, and influences that are foreign to, or even opposed to, our own. We also include the facets of our own personality, our qualities and our faults. With all these variables, it is impossible to foresee the slightest proportion between our efforts and our results.

In order to convert someone, we join sacrifice to prayer, we are gentle, yet our effort may seem wasted. Our conduct and our advances do not conquer indifference; sometimes even, our insistence drives that person further away from religion. On the other hand, a brief conversation with a stranger awakens a desire for the light or a secret remorse which will lead to that person's return to God. We tire ourselves out, while others harvest at the cost of hardly any effort. Nothing appears where one has sown laboriously, but elsewhere, one has only to stretch out one's hand in order to gather fruit.

God permits these paradoxical experiences in order to convince us that it is he who is at work. He requires our cooperation, but we are only the instruments with which he accomplishes his work. The result depends on him: we are not responsible for it. It is also always necessary to refer back to him: in success, to thank him before taking pride in it, and in defeat, to retain our trust in him.

Whether it be a question of education, instruction, or conversion, the agreement and voluntary effort of the people to whom we attend is needed in each case. It is God who awakens their desires, who keeps them alive, and who finally brings them to fruition—not us. Only he can magnify the soul.

GOD CHOOSES US TO HELP HIM

God nevertheless chooses to have people help him, and the fact that God uses us to help him carry out his plan is a wonderful feature of this world. It is not those who aid him who convert a soul, it is God. Our function is, first, to pave the way for divine action, then, when it has begun, to prolong and develop it.

Jesus compares these two periods of the apostolate with the two distinct duties of the sower and the reaper. It can happen that the same worker reaps what he has sown, and parents generally have the joy of seeing the fruit of their labors, although their reward is sometimes too slow for their liking.

If someone has returned to God because of our influence we may have reason to rejoice at it, but others had worked for his conversion before us. Others had sown the seed in this field, where we were only sent as harvesters. Some dead person, in heaven or in purgatory, had prayed for him, an unknown invalid had offered his sufferings for him, some book he read, the casual word of a friend, or the good example of a Christian had acted on him without his even noticing it. How many seeds there were that one could have thought were lost, carried off with the wind, but which had actually penetrated that soul by the slightest of openings, and been covered over at first by a thick layer of indifference, and apparently stifled by adverse passions.

You are mistaken when you say, "I have failed in the education of my children," or, "I have not been able to do good around me." What is important is that you have sown, that you have brought God to souls. When God wills it, these souls shall return to him. Perhaps you will not be there to see it, but others will reap where you have sown.

The true merit of the apostle consists less in reaping than in sowing. Now, we can always sow. To sow means to act, to talk, and to pray. It means above all living our Christianity frankly and to the full. The apostolate is the manifestation of a Christian life. It consists in saying the proper thing in the proper way, at the proper time. To sow is, finally, to pray. The absence of this condition of the apostolate can explain the delays that sadden so many well-intentioned tutors and apostles. To limit oneself to praying for others is usually not enough, for God demands direct action from us. But by praying for them, we bring God to them.

21

WITNESSES TO CHRIST

Many Samaritans from that city believed in him
because of the woman's testimony, "He told me all
that I ever did." (John 4:39)

The unexpected conversion of the village of Sichar
made an unforgettable impression on the disciples.
It must have seemed even more extraordinary to them
that the attitude of these Samaritans was so unlike the
welcome that the Jews gave our Lord.

The rest of St. John's Gospel shows the growing
hostility of those who reject Jesus as their Messiah. They
demand signs from him, they scrutinize his sermons,
they reproach him for having recruited poor people and
sinners. In four sentences, the Evangelist shows us here
the entirely different dispositions of Sichar. First, they
yielded to the testimony of a sinner. Then, in the Savior's
presence, they begged him to stay with them—and his
words would convince them that he was not only the liberator of Israel, but the Savior of the world.

These verses point out by what process souls can be led to the faith. Besides, in the art of bringing others to the faith, the believer strengthens it in himself. From this dual purpose point of view, it is worthwhile meditating on the conversion of the Samaritans of Sichar.

Note that their conversion comes first through the witness of Photina. Only when they hear Jesus do they reach the second stage, where they adhere to divine revelation.

They have not yet reached that stage when they are making their way toward Jacob's well. God is certainly guiding them there, but they have still made a mere act of human faith by believing the word of their fellow villager. Intrigued by her statements, they suspect the intervention of God in her sudden transformation. With her they repeat, "Is he not the Christ?" Without this initial goodwill, they would never reach total faith. Their goodwill is more than just a spirit of curiosity: it is a positive desire to know the truth that they may believe. Theologians call it the preambles of the faith. They take this step on *human testimony*. Let us examine this preliminary condition to the act of supernatural faith.

With few exceptions, the starting point of faith is a word from a friend. In the same way, those who have not received the benefit of a Christian education, and who come nevertheless to the faith, or those who return to it after a fairly long period of unbelief, do so under the influence of some human testimony. A book sets them thinking, a conversation disposes of some of their difficulties. But more than scientific demonstrations or kindly explanations, it is a Christian's life which gives them a foretaste of the truth of Christianity.

For it is not arguments that persuade in the first place, it is facts. We accept the arguments when the facts have already half-convinced us.

Just as the people of Sichar want to see the man who has wrought such a change in their neighbor, so too the unbeliever, the lost sheep, or the inquirer can no longer remain indifferent about the Christ whose image the true Christian offers them. So true is this that our Lord presents the apostolate to us as a testimony. At the Ascension he entrusts the mission in these terms: "You shall be my witnesses in Jerusalem and in all Judea and Samaria and to the end of the earth" (Acts 1:8).

The apostles will testify to his resurrection, to say that they have seen and heard him. They will also have to give the more intimate testimony of lives sanctified by the spirit of Jesus. Their piety, joy, and simplicity immediately earn them the favor of upright souls in the form of growing conversions.

If human testimony is the starting point of faith, it might be supposed that these witnesses should only be people qualified for this mission by reason of their authority, their knowledge, or their sanctity. This is not the case. Every Christian can and should be the witness of Christ. In this regard, the story of Sichar is instructive, for its inhabitants believed at the word of its least qualified.

Undoubtedly the lowliness of the first apostles was a great sign of the divinity of the Church. The weakness of the means used for conversion was a striking proof that God himself was at work.

THE SIMPLE LIFE

The Savior's choice was inspired, however, by a different motive. When one examines it a little closer, one sees that he could not have chosen anyone else. The simple life is the chosen territory of the gospel, only there can the fundamental virtues of Christianity appear and flourish. Greed for wealth is the greatest obstacle to the new spirit. Jesus denounces it constantly, because it keeps selfishness, cruelty, injustice, falsehood, hatred, and carnality alive in the heart of man.

That is why Jesus picks his apostles from among the ranks of the unimportant people whom the love of money has not yet perverted. This does not mean that he has banished the others from the Kingdom of Heaven. Far from it. The others will come in afterwards, but only in order to join the insignificant people, and they will bring to the gospel a more moving and rare testimony because they will detach themselves from the bonds of money and pride.

Our Lord could not do otherwise. Suppose twelve rich and pious Pharisees became his disciples, sold their goods and gave them to the poor. The poor would have admired this gesture, and eagerly sharing their spoils, they would have become attached to money. Other rich people would have been sure not to imitate such a useless gesture. In the end, no one would have understood the lesson of these original twelve apostles. Christianity would have become the prerogative of a class, a group of monks who were edifying but without any influence over the world.

History only confirms the tactics adopted by the Savior. In all ages and in every country, movements of evangelism recruited their first adherents among the middle classes, and won over little by little the camp of the powerful and rich, as the latter were won over themselves by the simple spirit of more humble brothers. Christ is always born in a stable, and his first worshipers are always the poor who have nothing, and then the rich who lay their treasures at his feet.

The indispensable condition of the first apostles is that they dispense with money. The apostle who betrays the Master's cause is Judas, the avaricious one. The true witnesses of Christ must be humble and detached. The Samaritan woman fulfilled this condition. But she had sinned, and the fact that Jesus used such a messenger was a great shock.

Yet Jesus did not choose his disciples solely from among those who had always led a holy life. He needed as a witness St. Peter, who blushed one day at being his disciple, St. Thomas who did not want to believe in his resurrection, St. Paul who began by persecuting the Church. Even St. John's fanaticism at one point drew the reproach of Jesus.

Is sin a requirement to lead sinners back to God? No, of course not. The Lord needs witnesses who have never offended against him. But he also needs some who bear witness that even the best can fall into error, so that such people will stay watchful. He also needs these others to bear witness that sin is not a prison of no escape. What sort of witnesses are we?

If we believe in him and love him, this testifies in his favor. But is it likely to persuade those who do not believe or love him because they have a false idea of him? Let us remember that people outside judge Christianity by what it has made of us.

22

PRAYER AND FAITH

So when the Samaritans came to him, they asked him to stay with them; and he stayed there two days. And many more believed because of his word. (John 4:40–41)

Jesus loves those who make straight for their goal. Could one have foreseen that things were going to progress so rapidly? The Sicharites certainly shared the prejudice of the Samaritans against the Jews. *Non coutuntur* (No dealings). Photina had objected when our Lord first spoke to her. She assured them that this Jew was not their enemy. Their prejudice collapsed and they came to him.

Contrast the Samaritans with the unbelieving Jews. They pester the Savior continually for some outstanding sign. They insist on seeing miracles. The Samaritans, on the contrary, do not demand a miracle from him to prove that he is the Christ. After all, to change a heart, to enlighten and purify a conscience, is that not a truly divine work? The conversion of their compatriot is sufficient miracle for them.

They only want to hear him, but they need more than a short conversation. The first words which they address to him are not like the suspicious questionings which Jesus had to put up with so often, they are a prayer. *Rogaverunt eum* (They asked him). They already trust him. They pray him to delay his departure, to stay, even if it is only for one night. Photina had no doubt told them of how weary he was when she had found him.

Without a moment's hesitation, Jesus agrees to stay. His disciples cannot get over their surprise. Their Master lets himself be surrounded by these strangers who are so eager for the truth, and who escort him to the village, attentive to his every word. They will shortly be contesting for the honor of offering him hospitality. It is only with regret that Jesus will leave them after having spent two days with them.

This mutual sympathy that is set up is one of the most mysterious elements of the faith and one of its indispensable conditions. A little earlier in St. John's Gospel, he gives an altogether different view of an earlier response when he speaks of Jesus' first stay in Jerusalem. "Many believed in his name when they saw the signs which he did; but Jesus did not trust himself to them; because he knew all men for he himself knew what was in man" (Jn 2:23–25).

Carried away by his miracles, the Jews had immediately recognized the power of God in him. But Jesus knows that they will ask him for what he will not give them, a material revolution. Instead he asks his disciples to change only the dispositions of their hearts. So almost all his first followers desert him and turn against him. The miracles which had suddenly caused them to believe are even more suddenly forgotten.

The people of Sichar are completely different. The sudden conversion of the Samaritan woman had prepared them to receive the faith. They do not lay down conditions for the Savior: it is they who ask him what his conditions are. They do not come as partisans motivated by preconceived ideas, but as disciples who dream only of listening, learning, and fulfilling. Jesus could believe in them and this is why he stayed in their village for two whole days.

In bringing together these two episodes, we are led to a conclusion of a more general kind: there are believers in whom Jesus does not believe; there are professions of faith which leave God unconvinced. And, on the other hand, there are people who think that they do not have the faith, who despair of ever being able to believe, but Jesus, who knows the capabilities of each person believes in them the whole time.

The true character of faith ought not escape us: it is not an intellectual adherence to a doctrine which seems to be true or maybe only plausible. Jesus does not ask his friends to estimate the value of his message and approve of its content. He says to them, "Believe in me." People do not believe in something; they believe in someone

Mark out the path that the people of Sichar followed to come to the faith. Human testimony has revealed Jesus to them: they want to see him. Having seen him, they are immediately conquered by him, before he has even spoken to them. They then beseech him. They pray that he will stay with them. His words do the rest: they have heard them, they believe.

This example should enlighten the Christian who is charged with guiding others toward the Christian faith.

People drawn to Christianity, whether through what they already know of it, or maybe because of a Christian's example, must first be led to Christ, made familiar with the gospel, brought into contact with Christian worship, and led to pray.

We should always get unbelievers who are truth seekers to pray. They would not be searching for him if God were not drawing them to himself. Prayer will favor their reconciliation with him. The prayer they can use may be found word for word in the gospel: *Domine, adiuva incredulitatem meam.* Lord, help my unbelief. Is there any appeal that could better touch God's mercy?

The inhabitants begin by asking Jesus to stay with them, then they listen to him. In the same way, one ought at least familiarize inquirers with the pages of the gospel that are most accessible to them. If they put themselves thus under the influence of Jesus, if they try to live according to the gospel, still by virtue of a simple human experience, little by little the Lord's doctrine will penetrate into their souls.

The lesson of Sichar ought not to be lost on us, the believers. The faith, like all the soul's noblest feelings, is an extremely delicate thing. It can, on certain days, seem less precise, a little undecided, or it may sometimes undergo a partial eclipse.

The believer also has the obligation to study in order to avoid these failings in his faith or to remedy them. But prayer is more necessary for us than study, and it can be confidently stated that failings of belief will not befall the Christian who keeps, without fail, daily contact with Jesus Christ. These include prayer, Holy Communion, and meditation on the gospel and on spiritual books.

But at the first uncertainty which troubles you, pray to Jesus, as the people of Sichar prayed to him, and later as did the two disciples at Emmaus, *Stay with us, Lord*.

Realize the divine presence of our Lord in your life. Force yourself to bring him more into your daily life. Meet him in your work, speak to him as to a traveling companion, see him seated near you at the family table. The feeling of his presence will give your conversations a better and more charitable tone. Your intimate thoughts will be inspired by his spirit, your affections will be stronger, your troubles lighter, his smile will cheer you when you wake up, and you will throw yourself on your knees to greet him with hope for the new day.

23

EXPERIENCE OF THE FAITH

They said to the woman, "It is no longer because of your words that we believe, for we have heard for ourselves, and we know that this is indeed the Savior of the world." (John 4:42)

The inhabitants of Sichar meant nothing offensive to Photina by this remark. On the contrary, all their lives they will thank her for having led them to Christ.

But what she had taught them about Jesus—that which was the beginning of their faith—had been so far surpassed by what the Savior had taught them himself. They simply say, "You did not lie to us, but the truth is even more beautiful than what you had told us."

This is how those who experience the faith will always reason. When the sinner is thanking the preacher who led to his conversion, he will not be able to stop praising the sweetness of divine forgiveness.

The experience of her people does not weaken Photina's testimony. It has added an irresistible light to it. Under the direct influence of Jesus, they give themselves over, body and soul, to him. No conversation, no books, and no examples need convince them other than the presence and action of Jesus.

This irreplaceable inner conviction can never exhaust itself. When a spirit comes to the truth, the truth dazzles, but this impression can weaken as the spirit becomes more accustomed to it. Such is the fate of those of whom Jesus was speaking and who limit themselves *to listening to his words*. The true believer, explains the Master, *puts his words into practice*. Not merely a respected preacher, Jesus is the well-loved Master whom his disciples follow at all times. In these circumstances, religious certainty no longer runs any risk of growing weak. Rather, it shows itself with an ever-increasing power.

One sees in the Samaritan woman an image of human authority, and even the Church's authority, on which our belief is necessarily founded. *Faith from authority* is indispensable, followed by *faith from experience*, acquired from spiritual communication with Jesus Christ, then from diligently receiving the sacraments, and then from the hardships of the Christian life.

Faith is based exclusively on God's revelation, but to be sure that God has spoken, we cannot rely on our religious experiences alone because of their strictly subjective character. Our intuitions can lead us astray; in any case, they are not equipped to discern the truth. The proof of this lies in the fact that among people with the most widely varying beliefs, one meets those who affirm with equal certainty that their dogmas and their rites have brought them into contact with God.

We need to be even more wary still of our emotions. One sinner will feel himself moved when he attends the first Holy Communion of his child; another, on reading a page of the *Imitation of Christ*. These impressions may be a direct contact with God, but they may just as well be a purely natural nervous phenomenon; in any case, they could not supplant the state of grace, nor furnish the slightest indication of it. On the other hand, some Christians who lead blameless lives and who never let a day pass without prayer can feel for some time a frustrating sterility in their prayer. They are nonetheless united to God, although they do not feel it.

It is just as risky to claim to base our faith on an inner enlightenment that may only be a case of self-suggestion. As for discovering a sign of God's favor or will in events that turn out to our satisfaction, these illusions can lead to disappointments and errors. The reasons that God can have for fulfilling our wishes or not are independent of the reasons for which we ought to believe in him. If the healing of a dangerously ill child is offered as a "proof" of the goodness of God, one would have to regard as a proof to the contrary the sorrow of a mother who sees her child die despite her most ardent prayers.

PERSONAL INFLUENCE OF JESUS

These examples prove that personal religious experience cannot be considered as a certain proof of the truths of the faith. With this in mind, we do need to *experience* the faith. This consists in putting ourselves under the personal influence of our Lord, Jesus Christ.

This faith, received with submission, is undoubtedly enough for our salvation. And so it is necessary to conserve it, to guard it against impiety, doubts which can disturb our minds, and temptations of pride, laziness, or sensuality. All of these make us avoid the obligations of our faith. They strike indirectly but surely at our faith itself.

Some people never suffer these attacks, others have to keep up a severe struggle in order to overcome them, while others, unfortunately, succumb to them. God does not leave us defenseless in this combat: this is when the faith of experience comes to reinforce the faith of authority, as we submit ourselves wholly to the action of divine grace that strengthens our faith, which makes of it a personal conviction against which all attacks will be in vain.

Each of us only has to cultivate this gift, by intensifying our friendship with our Lord Jesus Christ: He makes himself known directly to the person who believes in him and who loves him.

Furthermore, believers must do more than merely preserve their faith for the sake of not losing it. It is of value only insofar as it is put to good use. God has not made known to us the truths of religion in order to increase our knowledge uselessly or to offer us the opportunity of making an act of obedience and humility by accepting them. He means his truths to change our lives radically.

Complete faith implies living Christianity to the full, that is to say, the habit of submitting our judgment to the Christian truth, of practicing the evangelical virtues, of having recourse to the sacraments, and of taking an active part in liturgical worship. Thus religion is no longer imposed on our spirit just by the completeness of its traditional proofs. It becomes our thinking, our life.

24

THE SAVIOR OF THE WORLD

We know that this is indeed the Savior of the world.
(John 4:42)

I t is on this triumphant claim St. John ends his
account. *The Savior of the world*. The Samaritans of
Sichar understand the gospel better than the Jews. Up
to the very end, the latter want to capture the Messiah
for their nation's benefit. The faithful Apostles who
walk with Jesus on the morning of his Ascension, still
ask him, "Lord, will you at this time restore the kingdom to Israel?" The people of Sichar immediately had
a far broader and more accurate view of things. Jesus
could not be the prophet of one nation, the liberator of
one people: he is the *Savior of the world.*

Not even a few months had passed since Jesus' brief
stay at Sichar before doubts were already being expressed
elsewhere about his mission. St. John the Baptist heard
rumors of it from his prison and sent some of his own
disciples to Jesus with this message: "Are you he who is
to come, or shall we look for another?" (Lk 7:18–20). After

twenty centuries of Christianity, this question still presents itself to many people. It cannot be said, in fact, that the world is saved. People have not yet succeeded in halting injustice. It still produces the same evils, theft, and murder, with this one difference—the progress of science and technology makes them more atrocious and multiplies the number of victims. The reign of sin is not abolished. God is unknown.

Even if it is true that Christ's doctrine has been able to satisfy the most demanding intelligences, and that his morality has exalted the most generous hearts, are not the great majority still strangers to, or ill-disposed to, Christianity?

It is, of course, accurate to speak of the social character of the gospel, but many people make mistakes by looking to it for a code of political or economic obligations. Jesus refuses to be part of this plan. When they want him to make a political statement, he distinguishes between the clearly separate domains of God and of Caesar. And when one asks him, "Teacher, bid my brother divide the inheritance with me," Jesus replies to him, "Man, who made me a judge or divider over you?" (Lk 12:13–14).

Jesus is indeed a reformer, but his reform is an inner and religious one. Our Lord would not be the Savior if he had limited himself to patching up superficial sores. He had to get at the evil in its depths. This is why he did not address his attack toward institutions, but to human beings.

He shows deep indignation at social injustice, most evident in the parable of the rich man and Lazarus (See

Lk 16:19–31). Every time that a chance presents itself, he comes to the defense of those whose rights were unknown: the poor man, the child, the woman. But he takes care not to legislate. He leaves to his disciples the task of bringing appropriate, timely, and efficacious remedies to the injustices of their times.

When the Pharisees ask him when the kingdom of God was coming, he answers them: "The kingdom of God is not coming with signs to be observed; nor will they say, 'Lo, here it is!' or 'There!' for behold, the kingdom of God is in the midst of you" (Lk 17:20–21).

INTERIOR REFORM

The salvation which Jesus brings about in the world is not only an interior reform, it is above all a religious one. Jesus knows the cause of the profound evils that he must cure from within the human heart. He knows what has contaminated this hidden source of all evil, the revolt against God.

Let us suppose the existence of a human community, all of whose members were attached to God by the bonds of a filial and loving obedience. Would we not see bad feelings, rivalries, or, at least, hatred and violence disappear very quickly?

Some people challenge this idea, basing their argument on the unchanging wickedness of human nature. People, they insist, will always be either stupid or wicked, and you are going to give them the wonderful promises of the gospel? It is necessary that a determined

upper class, a strong man, should impose discipline.
Good laws will change bad customs little by little,
they say.

Others brush Christ aside by relying, on the contrary,
on the good inclinations of our nature. In their eyes, the
injustices of society are the only things responsible for
evil human feelings. If men, made better aware of their
true interests, came together in the worship of justice,
they would save themselves. But they must first free
themselves from the hindering influence of Christianity.
The gospel, they state, has slowed up the progress of the
world by fixing the attention and the hopes of men on
the after-life. Instead of preaching resignation to present
evils, let us build the future city here below.

All that these reformers lack is the means of creating
fraternity among the people who will always be divided
by their personal interests. Obedience to God is the only
means of achieving this spirit of brotherhood.

Heaven does not make us forget the earth. Jesus
promises the compensations of eternal justice only to
those who struggle and suffer here below for the sake
of justice. He only promises happiness without end to
those who devote themselves on earth to the happiness
of their fellow humans.

The mistake of believers is not in looking too much
toward heaven, but in not thinking of it often enough.
For in forgetting heaven, they let themselves be caught
up by the love of earthly goods, they let class interests
cloud over and stifle charity in them, and they tolerate
injustices when they benefit from them.

PERSONAL SIN

We can now reply to the objection with which we opened this discussion: why has Christianity changed the world so little? Because coming between humanity and happiness is the deep trench of all our sins. The evils that make us miserable come from our sinful tendencies.

Is this not a striking proof that we need a Savior? As long as he has not found Christ, man is a mystery to himself, because he feels that he is made to transcend himself and is powerless to do so. Left to itself, humanity falls unceasingly to the animal level from which God wishes to raise it. Sin is nothing other than the renewed fall of man who is raised up and then falls again.

There is only one efficient remedy: this is the one that Christ has come to bring to us, to snatch man from sin by making him dependent once more on God. Then will people love one another and the world will be saved.

EPILOGUE

THE SUPREME TESTIMONY

On the same day, the Saints Photina, a Samaritan, and her sons Joseph and Victor; also, Sebastian, military officer, Anatolius, and Photius; Photides, Parasceves and Cyriaca, sisters, who were all martyred for confessing Christ.

(Roman Martyrology, March 20)

When you have finished telling a child a story, it is not unusual for the young listener to ask, "And then what happened?"

For the child, a story is never ended, and he will not thank you for one as long as he does not know what became of the people you told him about. Closing the page of the Gospel in which St. John finishes the story of the Samaritan woman, we would willingly ask the holy writer the same question: And what happened afterwards?

Yes, what remained of the fervor of the inhabitants of Sichar? Did they stay faithful to Jesus or did they imitate the ingratitude of others? And more particularly, what happened to Photina? Did she fall once again into her old errors, or was she never thirsty again after Jesus had given her the living water?

As for Photina, we are better informed. Although further unmentioned in Scripture, at least the Roman Martyrology vouches for her perseverance. Not only did she keep her faith in Jesus, but she professed it at the price of her life.

In relation to the persecution ordered by Nero or to that of Domitian which followed it, we do not possess official records such as the Church published later on to the glory of its martyrs. Lacking first-hand documents, one can only believe in local traditions established quite a long time after the events, which do not have a strictly historical character. Those who wish to reject these traditions are free to do so; others who wish to cling piously to the memories that were handed down in every Church about those who died for the faith, are also free to do so.

The Church of Carthage took pride in the story of Photina's martyrdom. Without getting involved in the details given about the different persons listed after her, nor in the circumstances of their execution, let us note, at least, concerning her, that she brought her children into the Christian faith. More than thirty years after her conversation with Jesus at Jacob's well, so deeply engraved in her heart were the Savior's words that she answered them with the testimony of her blood.

When persecutions and wars compelled her to leave Samaria, she doubtless went, as on the day of her conversion, at the head of that little group of disciples who, believing that they were going into exile, went off quite readily to spread the gospel in the world. Did she come as far as Rome, as a Greek tradition claims? Should one, as a Spanish tradition holds, attribute to her the conversion of Nero's daughter, Domnina, whom, along with all her servants, Photina supposedly baptized? It does not matter. What does matter is that she brought Jesus to people, and after having lived in order to make him loved, she died for him with the same proof of her faithfulness.

But which should be the more admired, the irresistible power of Christ over a soul, or that soul's unshakable attachment to Christ? Among the number of signs by which the world should recognize his Church, our Lord includes martyrdom. He repeatedly predicts the murderous persecutions that will strike his disciples.

However, in predicting these sufferings, the Savior does not merely intend to strengthen his followers' courage. He sees something else in the violence of which they will be the object. He explains, "This will be a time for you to bear testimony" (Lk 21:13). The Greek word which means testimony has given us our word *martyrdom*. Martyrdom is the supreme testimony. But if Christ demands this proof by blood, what is the meaning and importance of such a testimony?

There are many false ideas expressed on this subject. One consists of seeing in Christian martyrdom a survival from the human sacrifices of idolatrous creeds. This is not so, since God gains no pleasure in breathing the bitter smell of our blood. If the God of the Prophets was already disgusted by the sacrifice of animals, all the more reason why he would not be eager for human victims.

The Church refuses the title of martyr to those people who deliberately expose themselves to death. The early Christians were forbidden to proclaim themselves as such to their enemies, or to provoke the pagans by outrages against the latter's cult. What is more, the Church approved, and even advised, flight during persecutions. The Christian should not be haunted by a constant thirst after death, for Christ has outlawed this indirect form of suicide.

Jesus knows that every measure will be tried against his work, and that in order to stop the gospel's spread, opposing powers will not hesitate to kill his disciples.

What will be, on the other hand, the object of this testimony? Here again, let us correct a common error. We do not claim that martyrdom proves the truth of Christianity because people would not let themselves be killed for a lie.

A testimony, properly speaking, relates only to facts. Christian martyrdom proves this basic fact: the appearance of the Son of God among mankind. All Christian martyrs bear witness to the essential fact that Christ has come into this world, that he has entered into their lives, that he has become the greatest love of their lives, that he alone gives them meaning. To the point that, if forced to choose, they prefer to renounce life rather than renounce him.

Certainly the martyr confirms his belief in a doctrine. In giving up the present life prematurely, he is certain that he will enter into the fullness of life, finding once more him for whom he is going to suffer. But if he is sure of this, it is because the Son of God has said so, and it is to this his death will testify.

In fact, in offering his life, the martyr proves that Christ's work is being continued in the world. He adds his sufferings to the Savior's in order to complete the redemption of the world. (This is why the church wishes that the Eucharistic sacrifice, which perpetuates that of the Cross, should take place on the tomb, or at least on the relics of a martyr, as if to mingle the blood of the Christian with that of Jesus Christ.) The death which the martyr accepts, although he did not seek it, shares in the value of Jesus' death, to which it joins. The martyr is not a disillusioned person who makes his escape from a world whose perversity sickens him. He is the conscious and joyous worker for the conversion of the world. He knows that from his death will come a renewal of life and holiness for the Church.

We conclude by admiring the heroic courage of this "cloud of witnesses" (Heb 12:1). But who can say what Providence has in store for us? Though martyrdom is a permanent condition in the Church, persecution and peace alternate to a rhythm that we do not regulate ourselves.

If we bear witness to Christ at the most easygoing times of peace, we shall do so at the time of a persecution. Let us often remember that in many Christian countries, our brethren are suffering cruel persecution. Let us pray for them and make our courage as great and strong as theirs.

By a virtuous life, by a noble apostolate, let us preserve in our hearts, as the Samaritan woman did, an ardent love for the Savior. Let us be from now on truthful witnesses of Jesus Christ.